GOD'S GUERRILLAS

The true story of Youth With A Mission

by

R. Marshall Wilson

Illustrations by Jim Howard

Logos International
Plainfield, N.J. U.S.A.

GOD'S GUERRILLAS

Copyright 1971 by Logos International
All rights reserved
Printed in the United States of America
Logos International, Plainfield, New Jersey 07060

Library of Congress Catalog Number 71-123999
ISBN 0-912106-10-7

Preface

One day, six years ago, I interviewed Loren Cunningham for a short article about his new group called Youth With A Mission. After he finished, I asked for another interview to get more "facts" for the story. This young man fascinated me. I couldn't believe he was real. He really lived what he preached. And I mean he preached it straight, like living a life totally committed to God's will.

By the next summer I was so interested that I went with a team of Youth With A Mission kids to the Samoan islands. They slept on air mattresses on the floor, ate canned food and piles of peanut butter sandwiches and walked all over the islands with the news that Jesus Christ died for every man's sins. During the last six years I've continued to follow them to countries all over the world. It's always the same story.

There are two things that have impressed me about the young people on YWAM. One, they are ordinary young people, not superholy. And two, they are determined to get the message out, no matter what it costs them in personal discipline. Sometimes it means walking miles in the burning tropical sun. Other places it is long, cold nights on the bare floor in a northern climate. They are a new breed of revolutionists, a movement of youth who believe the world can be changed without the sound of guns or bullets. I like to think of them as God's guerrillas, a valiant mobile band of strong youth.

So here are some of the lives of young people I have met personally in this movement. Please note that the first two fellows were given fictitious names. To tell the story of Don Clarke honestly, meant bringing up memories painful to many people he loved. Also, this part of his life is over. His name was changed so that we could tell you his story in truth.

Because Daniel Ivanovich's present ministry in Iron Curtain countries could be put in jeopardy through wide knowledge of his story, his name was also changed. The names of his grandfather and friend were changed as well. Several physical characteristics were altered for the same reason.

Youth With A Mission does not represent a denomination or church. It is open to Christian young people who want to change the world. Information about crusades and team opportunities can be obtained from Youth With A Mission, P.O. Box 4044, Burbank, California, 91503.

R. Marshall Wilson

CONTENTS

THE ACID MAN

Don Clarke sat staring at the draft notice in his hand. He was trying to figure out what to do. They would find him soon; he was still living near his parents' home. But what would the army do with him once they found him? He had used so much LSD now that he felt incapable of taking on a man's authority. He knew he could never discipline himself to army life.

Don looked over at Mary as she stood at the stove, fixing his dinner. Mary was the sweetest person he'd ever met. From the moment he saw her at a friend's house, he knew he loved her. She was married when she was fourteen and had two children. Her husband took her up north to the bush country. But he mistreated her so much that one day she couldn't take it any longer and just walked away, leaving the whole thing. Don rubbed his hand over the notice.

"I sure wish I could get away from all this," he said. "There must be some place in the world we could go and build a cabin and live a normal life. You know, raise some kids and grow our own food. Just exist together."

Mary turned and looked at him. "There's all kinds of room in Alaska. It's the perfect place to build that kind of home."

"Alaska." Don turned the word over slowly in his mind. That would be away from everything he had ever known. "Maybe I could even get off drugs," he mused half-aloud. "I'd like that. Just an honest, primitive life away from the world."

It was almost a year since he had started out on drugs and this trip to find reality. But now, even though he didn't like to admit it, he was getting frightened about his condition. Even his friendship with Terry had turned sour, and he thought that would never happen. They had been friends since they were kids. His mind went back to the afternoon last spring when Terry came walking up the school drive, that mysterious grin on his face, his red hair flashing in the sunlight.

"I've got something to show you," Terry said as he turned and fell in step with him.

"What is it?" Don asked. They stopped and Terry pulled his fist out of the pocket of his peacoat. Holding it down, away from the light, he opened his hand slowly. Three cigarettes lay in his palm.

"Joints," he said softly, that smile on his face again. "We've always shared everything in the past. I'd like to share this with you, too. What do you say?"

Don stood looking at them a moment. Terry was a special friend to him, a magic box full of surprises. There was always something new he could teach you about life, or women, or about almost anything. Now he was offering him another new adventure.

"Sure," said Don. "When?"

Terry put the joints back in his pocket. "Not now. You can't be acting funny around your folks. What about tonight?"

"Okay," Don answered.

He went home and tried to study, but his mind kept leaping ahead to the evening. He couldn't let his folks find out. His mom would go straight up. Mom never did like Terry. Ever since that day in third grade when she saw Terry hit him in the stomach, she hated him. Maybe that was part of why it was fun to run around with him. Terry was always saying that his folks were messing him up.

Don came back to the book. He'd better study. His grades were the lowest that he could remember. He was spending so much time with Nancy and trying to help her with her problems that his grades had fallen for the first time. Graduation was just a few weeks away and his folks were having fits.

After supper he told his folks he was going to the movies. Then he went out to his little sports car and drove over to Terry's house.

"Where do you want to go?" Terry asked as he climbed in.

"Oh, I don't know," Don answered. The two began to drive around town, looking for a quiet place without police. They went out by the lake first, but they remembered it was well patrolled. They cruised back through town, down to the wharf. That wasn't good either.

They were driving through a quiet residential area when Don pulled the car over and shut off the motor and lights. "What about this?" he said. "They probably don't come around here much."

"Okay," said Terry as he pulled out the joints. Slowly he lit the first one. "Now look, Don, this is the way you smoke it. Hold it this way so it won't burn you."

Don took the cigarette carefully.

"There, that's it. Now inhale slowly. There's nothing to be afraid of, it's really beautiful," Terry encouraged.

Slowly Don inhaled. Then he handed it to Terry. Back and forth they shared the joint until it was finished.

"Now," Terry said. "Just relax and wait."

The two sat quietly, waiting to see what would happen. Suddenly Don saw three sets of headlights come around the corner and shine on a hedge. Slowly, slowly the lights came toward them. They waited and waited, but the lights never reached them.

"Wow!" he said. Then he realized Terry had said it at the same time. They were experiencing the illusion together.

After that, whenever Don took marijuana, it was to share it with someone. At first, it was always with Terry and Terry's friends. Don decided he had found a new key in his purpose in life. He always wanted to share things, all his life. Share something with his friends that would bring them all together. Before he had shared through drink and sexual experiences. But now there was more.

Don and Terry began using marijuana as a replacement for liquor. It was a nice way to loosen up and forget their problems. Every once in a while, Don would get to feeling bad about what he was doing and go to confession. But it was just like he was going down the same checklist. He'd go out and pray with all the sincerity he could, trying to enter into the presence of God like when he was an altar boy. But within hours, he was back doing everything he had confessed. It was like he couldn't stop.

He and Nancy argued all the time now. But Terry insisted they were meant for each other, so Don continued to go with her. His grades kept getting worse, but he managed to graduate, mainly because of his previous record.

His parents gave him a trip to Hawaii for a graduation present. Terry gave him a lid of marijuana. The next day Don started packing. The first thing he got ready was a new surfboard. The second was a package of cigarettes to hide the marijuana in.

On the beach in Hawaii he met another guy with pot, so the summer stretched into strange days of adventures and illusions.

When he got back home, he made an effort to settle down into a normal pattern of living, but it was getting harder to do all the time. He enrolled in junior college because he needed to make up some credits before he could get into Maritime Academy. Nancy had faded away somewhere during the summer and soon he heard she was married. He was going out with different girls all the time, usually ones from Terry's group of friends.

He smoked grass constantly now, fifteen joints a day. He couldn't feel any urge to do homework. He'd start out the day going to class, but pretty soon he would skip out and meet his friends somewhere. They'd lie around on the grass, watching the clouds change shape, and talk about life. He was experiencing so many things now, all sorts of new ideas and sometimes deep conflicts. There were times when he began to feel lost, like he didn't know where he was. But then he discovered that he could get to a high on drugs where he didn't think about anything and he could just have a good time.

"I'm really escaping at last," he thought. "Now I'm experiencing people. It's more exciting than books on history or formulas for getting things done."

He was just floating along, learning all sorts of things, and having a great time. There was more to learn outside the classroom, so he dropped out of college. That fixed it with his folks.

"I just can't take any more of this," cried his mother. "We're going to leave our home and move away. Don't you realize what you're doing to us? Look at you!"

He went upstairs and looked at himself in the mirror. He

thought he looked pretty good. His hair was almost to his shoulders, a big change from the boy in the graduation picture in the living room.

He lay on the bed awhile. "What shall I do?" he asked himself. "I feel bad for the way I'm hurting the folks. But I'm stuck. I can't go back to what I was before, or I'll be defeating myself. I wasn't happy back there and I couldn't make my folks happy back there, either. But if I go on, I'll make them worse."

The last few weeks had been filled with constant family upheavals. His parents discovered he was taking dope. They took away his driving privileges as punishment. Then they took over his savings account, telling him there was too much money in it for him to throw away. Don shrugged. He had worked hard every summer to get the money but now it wasn't important. Sometimes they threatened to turn him in to the police. He just didn't care. He couldn't get scared about it. "You're just condemning me and my friends without giving us a chance!" he would end up yelling.

"Why don't you just leave home then?" his dad would counter, his mother in tears. Don determined to do just that. But there was something there that he couldn't break. Maybe it was because he was the youngest child and the only boy, but the bond between him and his folks seemed hard to break, especially the bond with his mother.

As he lay on the bed weighing the problem again, he finally saw that he was, in truth, enjoying his new life. Then it was no longer hard to leave his home.

He spent the days with Terry and the other new friends of the group. Occasionally he stopped by home and his folks gave him a little money. But he usually didn't need any. He would just drop in as sort of a houseguest to his friends. Some were still holding straight jobs so they had food and housing. They always had marijuana around their home and offered it to their guests like straight people offered a glass of wine.

Somewhere during this time, he didn't even remember when, Don started using acid. The neat thing was that each time he took it, he felt like he was getting closer to finding the key to reality. They had parties which didn't get going until everyone dropped so much acid that they would completely lose themselves. Then they would start a jam session or go for walks to watch flowers change colors. One night they chased invisible spiders.

Other times they sat around with pieces of cardboard. They drew pictures on it with felt pens and crayons. Then they drew something else on top of the old picture, using different colors. Over and over they embossed the cardboard, sometimes twenty or thirty times. Then they turned it over and looked at it. A new picture would appear on the back. They hung the artwork up on the walls. Months and months later, Don would go by a picture and see the same hallucination he'd seen the first time.

All this really amazed him. He was doing things he never imagined that he could do, just by letting his mind go. But there were other moments when he got scared. He had taken so much LSD that he had lost count of the trips. Terry was a big help during those times.

"Hey, man!" he said. "Look at the groovy things you're doing. There's a good life to be lived, Don, and you're living it!"

More and more he freaked out on his trips. Sometimes he felt like ants were crawling all over him. Once he stood on a cliff hundreds of feet above the ocean. The waves churning below looked inviting, and he felt an urge to go swimming. Slowly the water began to rise up until it was almost level to the cliff. He dove in. A ledge twenty feet down broke his fall.

Another time he was riding along in a car when he had this compulsion to get out. The driver didn't stop fast enough and he couldn't stand it. He put his fist through the windshield. The next thing he remembered was running through a field, screaming and screaming.

Life was a little more pleasant after he met Mary. He knew that if they were to live together he would have to get a job. But he didn't mind. He went to work as a garbage collector. Except for the fact that his long hair always caught in the handle of the big can he carried, he enjoyed the work. It was kind of pleasant out in the streets early in the morning, watching the straight people hurry off to work. He and Mary picked through each load of trash and salvaged usable furnishings which they fixed up for their little apartment.

Now Don looked around their little home. It was okay but his old life kept interrupting, like this draft notice. Slowly he stood up and crumpled up the paper.

"Okay, Mary," he said, "let's go to Alaska."

II

Don bought an old car and packed it up with a few belongings. Then they drove over to his folks' house to tell them good-bye. "You can't keep on like this," his mother said, trying to hold back tears. "You've got to end this way of living."

Don wondered how to answer her. He wanted to tell her he was sorry for the pain he was causing, but he couldn't explain the determination within him to keep on going. There just was no answer.

They stopped for a while in San Francisco, California. There they met some other young people who told them of a ranch where they could live the kind of life they were seeking. It was near Santa Rosa and it was called Morning Star. Don decided to check it out before going further.

It was raining when they turned off the highway onto the muddy road that led to the ranch. The car sloshed through the ruts. A strange feeling came over Don, like this was the end of the line. But his mind was too foggy to worry about answers.

Suddenly, a huge cross loomed up in the road ahead. It was implanted right in the middle of the muddy track. Maneuvering the car over to the edge of the road, Don felt the wheels slip and the car slide about while he gunned the motor to make it through.

The large ranch was owned by a professional musician who had dropped out and bought the ranch to share with people like him. There were five houses constructed as far as the framing and roof, but unfinished inside. Other people lived in the various sheds and ranch buildings as well as in some tents out in the meadows. Don and Mary lived in their car, waiting for an opening in the other shelters.

Morning Star was the most beautifully weird place Don

had ever seen. There were crosses everywhere, great tall ones on the green hillsides and even one on top of the little roof that sheltered the old well. The kids would put flowers on some of them every day.

One couple, Jim and Sandy, would sit around in their home and read Scriptures from the Bible every night after supper, just for the aesthetic nature of it. Jim liked things about God. He had a huge board against one of the unfinished walls of the house. He had painted a picture of St. Francis of Assisi on it and written his prayer beside it. Sandy was a Christian before she came to Morning Star. Jim left a common-law wife and five kids to start a new life here.

There were people of all ages living like one big family. When someone got money from home or sold drugs in town, it was put in the community fund and used for living expenses. Others would donate their food stamps, social security, unemployment, or child support checks so that they all could benefit.

By late March, when the green meadow was filled with wild flowers and the days were getting warm, Don and Mary moved into a vacant tent. It was out in the apple orchard with a nice cooking area. But something had happened to them. The magic was gone from their relationship. There was nothing new for them to experience emotionally, physically, or mentally. Mary began to drift off with other fellows on the ranch. Finally she moved out.

Don stepped up his drug intake to take away the hurt. One day he was sitting out in front of his tent when Mary walked by with some guy. They were talking and then she turned and laughed at Don. The drugs weren't enough. Her scorn went like a knife deep inside, and Don knew that he still loved her more than anything on earth.

Now Don withdrew completely to himself. It seemed like too much effort to reach out to anyone, even through speech. All day long he wandered about, lost in daydreams. He spent the time watering his little garden and playing with the rabbits in the hutches nearby. He was chain-smoking regular cigarettes and drinking, as well as continuing his drugs. It was a continual high now, without any kind of drive or motivation.

"Some people were lying around, playing guitars and enjoying the warm sun."

Once he wandered over by the owner's cabin. Some people were lying around, playing guitars and enjoying the warm sun. He stood there naked, watching the scene. A big bearded fellow came by and went over to the well. He was so drunk that his body was almost liquid. Don watched him as he slowly picked up the lid of the well and dropped it down inside. Then the guy leaned over to watch it fall, putting his hand across to the other side to keep himself steady. But his back sagged and he fell in, falling thirty feet to the bottom.

Don stood there, aware that the sun felt nice and warm on his back, while a gang converged on the well, trying to help. Somebody ran over and dove in with a rope. Still Don watched, unable to find the motivation to move and help. They finally lifted him out.

One evening in late April, Don came back from visiting friends at another commune and went straight to Jim's house since that was where he had enjoyed himself last.

He stopped outside the doorway for there was a stranger inside, facing a group of kids. She was reading from the Bible and talking about God. Don took a long look at her. He hadn't seen anyone like that for nearly two months. She was all that he had turned off. She was short, plump, and middle-aged, wearing patent leather shoes and carrying a big, patent leather purse. Her hair was brilliant red.

He couldn't follow what she was saying fast enough to understand, but she spoke with unusual power and yet with genuine love. "Wow," Don thought. He had never seen anyone like this before. She was real. He wanted that reality in his life.

The woman got ready to leave. Before she did, she turned and began to pray for a girl in the room. Don could feel the power of the woman's prayer as she spoke. He felt like he was about to find something.

He came into the house and walked near the woman, his eyes never leaving her face. She turned and looked at him. Her eyes were full of authority, yet warm and sincere. "You want me to pray for you, don't you?" she said.

Don stood there looking at her, smiling the same, weird way he always did since beginning acid. He couldn't make an audible sound, yet in his heart he answered yes.

The woman must have sensed what he thought because she spoke. "We're going to pray for you, that you will be delivered from demonic power."

Don stood there as the woman put her hands on his throat and began to pray. "I rebuke the spirit of dumbness in you, in the name of Jesus Christ!" she said. "You *will* say the name of Jesus and you will say it in a mighty witness of the Holy Spirit. You will speak of the name of Jesus to those who are hungry to hear it and you will speak of His redeeming love and His shed blood."

Something started to well up inside Don. It felt like the name of Jesus was letters like in alphabet soup. It would come together and form in his chest, and his heart would be yearning to say it. Then as it came up to his throat, it stopped. Something was keeping the name from coming out of him.

After the woman prayed for him and left, the people began to tell him about her. She was a former alcoholic and she came out to the ranch often to give Bible studies in this house. She was from a local church and she had invited some of them to attend her class on Sundays, which they did.

Several days later, Don was going past the house again when Sandy came out, a Bible in her hand.

"Hi," she said. "Some of the kids are going to church. Do you want to go with us?"

Don turned and began walking up the hill with her to where the cars were parked. When he came to the church, he saw that the world had kept on going without him. He hadn't seen so many straight people in months. He looked down at his faded Levi jacket and jeans. He became aware that his long hair was matted and standing on end and that his beard was dirty. The soles of his shoes flapped noisily as he walked inside to sit down with the rest of the group.

Some people sitting near him turned around. Then they smiled, like they really liked him. He hadn't felt that kind of love in a long time. The service got going and it was really groovy. The church was conducting a missionary crusade so it was filled with flags and posters. A huge banner hung from the ceiling across the choir loft. It read, "Multitudes, Multitudes in the Valley of Decision." The people sang and sometimes they clapped to the rhythm of the song. Don followed along, clapping and singing.

Then the pastor introduced the speaker. His name was Bernard Johnson and he was a missionary to Brazil. He was a fiery kind of speaker. Don was fascinated. It sounded exciting even though his mind couldn't grasp what he was saying. Then Don saw that everyone was standing up and waiting. The man was asking those who wanted to receive Jesus Christ to come forward.

When Don heard the name of Jesus again, that same strange desire began to well up inside. He saw somebody walk down to the front. Maybe he could go forward, too. The thought came, but there was no motivation. Finally he said in his mind, "Well, I'll do it." And he stepped out into the aisle.

When he got to the front he knelt right at the middle of the altar, his back straight and his head bowed with hands folded, like when he was an altar boy. He began to try to find God. As he waited, he sensed the presence of God like when he was a child. With the presence came an awareness of the attitudes he had carried in his heart and of the motivations which he had let rule his life. He sensed that these would have to go before anything could happen to him.

"All right, God," he prayed silently in his heart. "I've done everything I thought was right to do in searching for reality. But I've hurt You. I've hurt my parents. I've hurt everyone I've come in contact with and I can see I'm really wrong.

"Well, God," he went on. "I know that now is the time for You to lead me and I'm finally here. I want to ask You to help me now and just do what You want to do for the next step."

Don felt a man's hand on his head, the hand of a deacon in the church. The man began praying. "In the name of Jesus Christ, I rebuke you, Satan!"

It felt like an earthquake passed from the man's hands into Don's head. His whole body started shaking uncontrollably and he fell over prostrate on the floor. For a while, he wasn't aware of anything. Then he began to hear voices around him. The man was still rebuking Satan. He recognized the voice of the woman who prayed for him at the ranch. She was pleading the blood of Jesus Christ over him.

About half an hour went by with the people praying. Then, suddenly, Don felt a great surge developing inside him like something was moving. It was a weight, a huge, heavy weight, and it started oozing out like it was going out the pores of his skin. It was thick, heavy, and dark. And then, in a rush, it was gone.

Don couldn't move. He was empty inside. Absolutely empty, like a vessel with everything poured out. The people were still praying and pleading the blood of Jesus Christ over him. Slowly, a wonderful sweetness seemed to be coming in his nose and mouth, like the breath of life was being breathed back into him. He felt like a balloon that was being filled with a melting, honey kind of life.

When he opened his eyes, the first thing he saw was his hand. It was white and smooth, like it was brand new. Everywhere, inside and out, he was pure. Not a trace of darkness anywhere. His whole body was trying to move now. Slowly he got up off the floor and raised his hands in the air as he began to speak. His words were praises to God.

The missionary came over to him and asked him to renounce Satan. After he did, the man asked, "Who is Lord of your life?"

From out of the depths of Don's being came his answer. "Jesus Christ is the Lord of my life."

III

On the way back to the ranch that night, the kids stopped at a gas station to buy gas and cigarettes. Don took one and went to the restroom to smoke. For the first time, it bothered him to smoke. But at the same time, something inside was demanding it. Each time he took a drag, his hand started shaking. He realized that he couldn't stop smoking if he wanted to.

He began to pray. "God, I know that you did something in my life tonight. It was magnificent." Then he went over to the mirror and looked himself in the eye. "All right, in the name of Jesus Christ, stop smoking." The desire left him for good.

Wednesday afternoon, Don's parents arrived at the ranch. Shortly after he came to Morning Star, they had found out where he was, so they kept in touch, often sending him money. Now they went for a drive to get some hamburgers. They stopped at a park to eat them. Don began to tell of his new experience. When he finished, he was aware of another new desire.

"I think I want to cut my hair," he said.

His folks looked at him wide-eyed. "That's fine son," his dad said, "but we don't want to force you into anything."

"You're not," Don answered. "I really want to."

They got in the car and drove till they found a barbershop. Don sat watching his hair fall to the floor, waiting for some emotion to hit him. "Well, it's happening," he thought.

Afterward, his parents stopped in front of some stores. "Don," said his mother "what do you want? Is there anything we can get you, anything your heart desires?"

Don thought a moment. "I'd like a piece of cheese."

That afternoon Don took his folks to meet the pastor. They talked awhile and all came to the conclusion that it would be better for Don to live in a different environment from the ranch. But they also understood that it wouldn't be best for him to return home yet. He wasn't ready to meet his old friends or take up life with his parents.

So the pastor invited Don to live with his family for a while. Don's folks helped him move into the parsonage before they left. Four other boys from the ranch had become Christians. One day the pastor took them all down to the rescue mission where they were given suits. Don had a nice suit, white shirt, and tie given him. They also gave him a belt with a "C" on it and a new pair of shoes. Then he got out his everyday clothes that he had packed away at the ranch and never used.

His new life got better and better. The pastor and his wife would help him understand the parts of the Bible that he read each day. He just couldn't learn about everything fast enough to satisfy the hunger inside. Every time he didn't understand something and then someone would explain it to him, he would just sit there and say, "Wow!"

One of the special times to him was family devotions.

Watching this family, seeing the love that the pastor and his wife had for each other and then watching them together with their children, was a unique pleasure to him. He felt that he was seeing the reality of his dream of a perfect life at last. Now he saw that a person really could achieve it.

During the first week, Don attended the services every night. He would always go up to the altar afterward so he could pray with other people there. One night a lady came up to him. "Would you like us to pray that you will receive the Baptism of the Holy Spirit?" she asked.

"Sure," he said. "Go ahead." He didn't know much about it, but he wanted all he could get of this new life. So a group of people laid their hands on his head and asked the Lord to give him the gift of the Holy Spirit.

Don promptly sank to the floor, and for about forty minutes he lay on his back, praying. He would feel his spirit coming up inside him, like he was being carried up high. Then a question would come to his mind. "Will you give up everything?"

"No," he answered in his heart. Then the Spirit would sink back down. "No, no, I want it," he said then, for he realized that he was losing it. Again the Spirit would begin to rise up. But when the question would come again, he couldn't say, "Yes."

About the fourth time this happened, Don saw a vision. He was speaking to a crowd of people, telling them about Christ. "No," he said. "God, I don't want to do this."

Now the memory of how he knelt at the altar on Sunday night came back to him. He remembered how he admitted to God that he had ruined his own life. Now he saw that he had committed his life to God with certain reservations and God wanted him completely.

He hesitated another moment and the vision came to him again. "Okay, God, I give up," he said. "You can really have all my life, all of my heart."

Suddenly a wonderful sensation filled him. He was speaking in a language he didn't understand but the words seemed beautiful to him. He began singing while he glorified God in his heart. "So this is it," he thought. "I was seeking tongues, but it didn't come until I began to seek God Himself."

He declined a ride home that night, just so he could be alone with God. The moon was shining in the clear air and he sang with a new joy inside. The joy was still there in the morning when he awoke and it continued through the day.

It was the strength of the Holy Spirit which continued to help him a few days later when he discovered that the problems created in his old life hadn't disappeared. He was over at a Christian's home one night, where some of the other young people who left the ranch were staying. Don was talking on the phone when Mary and two friends walked in the door.

"I've heard about all this joy that you people are receiving," she announced. "And I want some."

Don grabbed the first guy he found and went outside. "Let's pray," he said. He wanted Mary to have this experience more than anything.

Mary did accept Jesus Christ into her life that night. She moved away from the ranch and began wearing dresses instead of jeans. She looked wonderful. Don knew in his heart that she was still married to someone else, but it was difficult to remember when he was with her. He turned the problem over and over in his mind, seeking guidance from people in the church and searching the Bible for answers.

One Sunday afternoon, Don and Mary were alone for a few moments, sitting in the back seat of a car. "As far as I can see," Don said finally, "according to God's Word it is your duty to go back to your husband. We shouldn't have a relationship with you married. But you must make the decision."

That night, Mary knelt at the church altar for a long time. A week later she boarded a bus for the North. Don's only comfort was his knowledge that he was standing for something right and not giving in to his emotions, a big step for him.

The pastor seemed to know what he needed during those days and put Don to work helping him build a little home missions church out of town. Each day was filled with new adventures in learning. He even had to learn how to use a fork again. One of the things he liked to do best was stop and talk to people about his new experience. He felt like he had to share it with everyone, for it was the most wonderful thing he had ever discovered.

One day the pastor came to him. "I think we've found a place where you could have a real ministry this summer."

Don looked up, delighted. This life was getting better all the time. "Where?"

"It's with a group of young people called Youth With A Mission. Young people dedicate their summer vacation to going door-to-door in foreign countries with the Gospel."

"Wow!" Don sighed.

IV

Don's parents released the money in his savings account to pay his way. So just two months after he found Christ, he was on his way down to the island of Trinidad with a team of young people. He took part in training crusades in Illinois and Ohio which helped him a lot.

Trinidad was another daily adventure for him. The days were filled with walking and talking to people about Jesus Christ. Sometimes it would be on a street corner, other times in the shade of a porch. Once he got to give his testimony to a group of Moslems at a mosque. Later, a young man came to the team's headquarters. He confessed he was a Christian but had become involved with the daughter of a high-ranking Moslem. Therefore he had started to worship with them. He recommitted his life to Christ and went out witnessing with Don in the afternoon.

In the evenings Don and the team would usually be in some sort of service, either in a church or an open-air meeting to reach the people wandering the streets. In his spare moments, Don studied the Scriptures, taking careful notes of each new revelation he got. At the same time, he began to learn how to discipline his life again by keeping up with the regular schedule of the team's daily work.

As Don sat packing his suitcase to come home at the end of the summer, his mind went back to the weeks in Trinidad. He really enjoyed those warm, sun-drenched days. And the people were open and interested in listening to what he had to say about Christ. He thought again of the faces of those who gave their lives to Christ. Yes, it was worth giving up all of his life to Christ, he decided. He had found that warm, full life which he sought on drugs and at the ranch.

All through his life his drive had been to share his experiences and himself with people. But it never turned out right. Now he saw the secret. He was sharing still, but he was sharing the life of another man, one who died for all men's sins. He had found the real Morning Star. It was a person, not a place. And that Person had come and brought light to his heart. He had found the key to reality at last.

RUSSIAN FUGITIVE

Dan stood looking at the deputy whose head was already bent over a blank form on the desk. "Name?" said the officer in the flat, bored tone of routine.

"Daniel Ivanovich."

"What's your address?" the officer went on, his pen moving from line to line.

"Ninth Avenue, San Francisco," Dan answered, shifting nervously. He'd better get control of himself. He didn't want to act like he was scared.

"Height?" asked the man.

"Five feet, six inches," said Dan.

"Weight?"

"One hundred thirty-five."

The officer glanced up. "Color eyes?"

"Brown."

"Hair?"

"Black."

The head went back down, the pen kept moving. "Give me the date of your birth."

"November, 1947," Dan said, his heart pounding in his ears.

"Place of birth?" asked the man.

Dan gulped. "China," he said softly.

Now the policeman's head shot up. "You don't look Chinese. Your folks missionaries or something?"

"No, sir," answered Dan.

The man didn't move. Dan knew he would have to explain. "My folks were Russians," he said.

Now the policeman's eyes narrowed. "What are you doing here in the U.S.?"

Dan took a deep breath, trying to calm down inside. "They were part of a group who left Russia just as Communism was taking over. They crossed over into China and lived near the border there during the Second World War.

Afterward, they came to the United States."

"Hmmph," said the policeman and went back to finishing the form. "You're being booked for petty theft. You're entitled to a couple of phone calls as long as you've got the money. Otherwise, I'll lend you a dime to call collect."

Dan shook his head. The last thing he wanted right now was for his folks to hear about this.

Later he sat in the jail cell, staring at the bare cement floor. For the first time since he could remember, he was really scared. It seemed like he had been hurtling down a road and now, suddenly, he had come to a halt. He was really in jail. And not for religious observance like his Grandfather Illyi had been in Russia, but for a crime.

"Not that it was all that bad," he thought, his mind returning to the events of the evening. He and his buddy, Jonathan, along with another guy, were stealing gas from cars at an apartment house when some man came out and saw them. The guy jumped into his sports car and began chasing them. They finally shook him during a wild ride up and down the steep hills of the city. What they didn't know till later was that he got their license number and reported them to the police.

Dan and the fellows drove on up to Sacramento, dragging with cars along the way. By the time they got there, they needed gas again. After cruising around they saw a car in a driveway so they pulled up and piled out. They had a lightning-fast system but a police car with lights out had been tailing them for hours. Dan saw the police finally, and they broke and ran. But it was too late.

"I wonder if Jonathan's scared," thought Dan. The two of them had come to America with their families when Dan was four years old. They lived near each other in San Francisco and went to church and school together until Jonathan's family moved away.

When Dan was in seventh grade, Jonathan moved back. "Hey, how come you don't go to church anymore?" he asked Dan right away. "You sure aren't living right. What do your folks say?"

"Aw, come on, Preacher," Dan retorted. "Knock it off. Listen, why don't you join our club? We've got a neat thing going."

Dan didn't want Jonathan to know it, but he was hoping that Jonathan would do him some good. But instead, Preacher talked less and less of God and entered into the gang life more and more.

One night Dan's gang decided to take revenge on another club that had broken into their clubhouse. What made them really sore was that the other gang had taken some of the stolen goods that the boys were hiding there. After it got dark, Dan and the fellows went to the home of one of the gang members. Without a sound they spread tubes of glue on the porch. Then they dropped lighted matches on it and ran. Dan looked back. It was an inferno. Anyone trying to get out of the house that way would burn to death. For a moment it bothered him. Then he shrugged and ran off with the rest.

As Dan and Jonathan grew older, they slowly dropped out of the gang and began to run around with a different bunch of guys. Jonathan was two years older than Dan so his friends knew a lot more about life and had some pretty exciting things to do. The two began drinking with the rest of the guys. It wasn't long until Dan saw that he could never drink much because Jonathan would always get so drunk that Dan would have to take care of him. Up until then, Jonathan was an excellent student in school. But he became so obsessed with drinking that he dropped out of high school.

For a moment, the thought that he was responsible for Preacher's condition came to Dan's mind. "No," he said to himself. "He knows what he's doing. I haven't done anything. Besides, I'm in as much trouble as he is. What if they keep us here for months?" Maybe he should have phoned his folks. No, he decided. It wasn't worth the risk.

For the first time in many, many months, Dan bowed his head and prayed. "God, if you get me out of this, I'll stay clean and all."

II

The next morning when the policeman came in and told Dan that he could go home, he thought his prayer had been answered. He was starting to relax inside when the man spoke again.

"We'll be getting in touch with the juvenile authorities in San Francisco about this, and they will be talking to your parents."

Dan gulped but then tried to play it cool so that Johathan wouldn't see. For days after that, every time he saw a car drive up in front of the house or when the phone rang, he would freeze inside, waiting for the news to come. But nothing happened. "I think I've made it," he decided one day as he returned home from school. But when he walked in the door, he knew this was it.

Everyone was crying, even Grandfather Illyi. It was worse than he imagined it would be, standing there unable to look at the hurt in their eyes. He knew that telling them he was sorry wasn't enough. They just couldn't understand why he did such a thing. Up to now he had assumed that they knew he was getting into trouble when he stayed out night after night. "But they didn't," he realized. "They were blind to all I've been doing these last couple of years. It didn't occur to them that I was different from Nick." That's what he got for having a big brother who was good all the time. Boy, he wished it hadn't happened. Man, if he could just forget the look on their faces.

Dan rolled and tossed into the early morning hours, the knot in his stomach too tight to let him sleep. Why couldn't they understand that he wanted to be a normal American boy? Grandpa standing there, not saying a word. But the look in his eyes!

All Dan could remember was Grandpa always taking him and the rest of the kids to the park, sitting there under the trees, telling them stories about Russia. Then time after time telling him, "Dan, you are meant to be specially used by God. This is why God gave you life again when it was gone. Never, never forget this."

Dan sat up in bed, jamming his fists into his eyes, trying to blot out his thoughts. He got up and stood looking out the window. Everything was quiet now outside. The fog was swirling around the street lights, making it a different world. His mind jumped back to the foggy Saturday mornings when they were kids.

The five of them would come into the folks' bedroom where they'd pile on the bed, begging for a story. Then Dad or Mom would start in, telling them of some adventure from their times in Russia or China. Everyone's favorite story was about the time Dan nearly died. Mom always told that one.

"Dan was only about three months old," she would begin, her soft brown eyes smiling. "We left Kuldja and were traveling across China to Lanchow. It was winter and very, very cold."

The kids would shiver in excitement and pull a blanket up around them. "Much of the time we had to travel in horse-drawn wagons," Mom continued. "So we sat in the rain and snow all day long. Then at night, many times there would be no building to sleep in so we stayed in shelters made out of straw.

"One day," Mom went on, her voice becoming low and serious, "Dan got the measles and broke out in a bright red rash. For many days he cried and wouldn't eat. When the rash went away, he was worse than before. I tried to keep him warm by carrying him inside my coat, but still he cried.

"For three weeks he was this way. We got to Lanchow and they told us about an American missionary hospital. We took Dan to them and they began feeding him through the veins, but still he got no better.

"I stayed there with the baby. One night when Grandfather and Papa came to see us, the nurse came in. She felt Dan's pulse and shook her head slowly. 'His pulse is gone,' she said. 'You better be ready for him to die.' So Grandpa and Papa went home to look for wood to make a coffin."

Mama would always stop the story here because all the kids would be sniffling, trying to hide their tears. "There, do not cry," she would say. "Look, Dan is here. Listen and it will be all right.

"Before Papa and Grandpapa built the coffin, they called together some of the Christians to pray. I was back in the hospital, watching Dan as he lay on his back in the crib. Suddenly, he flipped up into the air, out of the crib, and down to the floor, just like a fish! That's what he looked like, just like a fish jumping out of water." The kids would all squeal then.

"Was he all right, Mama?" his sister, Riassa, would ask.

"Oh, I was so scared," Mama went on. "I picked him up and ran to the hall calling the nurse. Well," Mama finished, breaking into a wonderful smile, "the nurse felt his pulse again. Then she said to me, 'His pulse is good now. He is much better.' And you see, he did get better. Look at him now!"

The words hung over Dan as he watched the fog. "Yeah, look at me," he thought. He sure hadn't done much with his life. He wished something would happen to him so he could be better.

The next morning at breakfast, Nick looked at him and said, "Dan, I'm going to do some stuff around town today. Why don't you come along?"

"Sure!" said Dan, glad to get out of the house and flattered by Nick's sudden attention to him. From then on, when Nick was doing something special, he'd often invite Dan to go with him.

One Sunday morning Nick said, "Why don't you go to church with me today?" Dan thought about it a minute. Nick was going to an English-speaking church. No one would know about him there like they did at the Russian church where his family went.

"Okay," Dan mumbled and went to get ready.

The service wasn't bad. In fact, he liked it enough that he decided to go again that night. He didn't remember much about the service afterward because all through the evening, such a deep sense of conviction weighed on him he couldn't even concentrate on what the visiting missionary was saying. The people stood and an invitation was given for those who wanted Jesus Christ to come forward. Dan took a deep breath and plunged down the aisle.

"Dear God," he prayed, unable to hold back the tears that had knotted inside him for so long, "please forgive me. Please come back into my life and help me live right."

III

Life was different now for Dan, and sometimes it wasn't too easy. Like during lunch hour. Before, he was always busy.

The guys always had something going, like stripping cars or taking motor scooters for joyrides.

Dan forced himself to walk to the woodshop and find something to do with his hands while he ate lunch. But they were lonely hours, and Dan felt it keenly. He wished he could get used to the way Christian kids lived. They got together on Sundays and sometimes in the middle of the week. But that was all, except for a party now and then.

"What do they do the rest of the time?" Dan wondered. Seemed like he was always hunting for some way to fill up his days.

One day at church, Paul Bruton, the Youth Director, came up to him. "Dan," he smiled, "I've been wondering if you would like to come down here on Saturday mornings with Steve Tedrow. We could get together and talk about spiritual problems and pray for some of the kids who don't know the Lord. What do you think?"

Dan felt a big relief rolling up inside him. "Yeah," he said. "I'd like that." Every Saturday the fellows would meet with Paul and share their problems, binding together in prayer over them. Shortly after that, one of the fellows they were praying for gave his life to the Lord and joined the Saturday group.

One day in spring, Dan came to church to hear a special speaker. He was a missionary-evangelist named Loren Cunningham. The young man told of plans to take a group of young people to the Bahama Islands and Dominican Republic during the summer. The kids would have to pay their own way. They would live simply, eating inexpensive food and sleeping on air mattresses, so that the cost could be kept low. They would spend the days going door-to-door, telling people about the work and person of Jesus Christ. The group was called Youth With A Mission.

"Wouldn't it be neat if I could do something like that?" Dan thought.

The next Saturday, Paul referred to YWAM while they were talking. All three boys sat up with interest. One after another told how something had spoken to his heart while Loren spoke. Each wished that he could go on such a venture. Then Paul confessed that he, too, wanted to take part.

They grinned at each other and began to pray.

As summer approached, each Saturday morning became the high point of the week. Someone always had news now of some little miracle that moved another obstacle out of the way. By the end of school, their finances had all worked out and each one made plans to go to Dallas, Texas, for the kickoff crusade.

A church bus picked up young people in California and drove them to Texas. When the bus stopped in Hayward, Dan saw an old buddy, Nick Anderson, get on. That made him feel even better about the trip..By the end of the first day of traveling, everyone in the crowded bus was talking and singing like old friends.

The first morning in Dallas, Dan took notes like crazy during the training session. He didn't want to mess up when he faced people at their homes. He managed to stay calm until it was time to go out. The young people were separated into teams. Then they were put into pairs to go door-to-door. Now Dan got really nervous. The thought of going out into a strange situation, with a strange person beside him, really got his heart going in his ears. They began reading off the names on Dan's team. "Dan Ivanovich will go with Nick Anderson."

"Neat!" he sighed and smiled at Nick. "Look, I'm not used to doing this, so you go ahead and talk at each house, and I'll be the silent prayer partner."

That was really a close call, he decided as they walked out the church door. He could relax now with Nick.

For several hours the two walked from house to house on a Dallas street. Near the end of the afternoon, they were walking up to a home when Nick said casually, "Dan, I'm tired of talking. You do it here."

Dan could feel his eyes getting big. "Aw, come on, Nick," he smiled. "Not here. Just one more house, please? I need to listen some more to how you do it."

"No," Nick smiled back. "This is your house, Dan. You're going to get up there and do all the talking."

Dan took a deep breath. He couldn't let Nick see how scared he was. Okay, he would just go up there and do it. There was nothing to get panicky about. He marched up to the door and knocked, with Nick standing behind him. The door swung open and a big Texan stood there looking at him.

"Hello," Dan smiled. "My name is Dan . . . Dan . . . Dan . . . " He was shaking so bad that he couldn't finish.

Concern filled the man's face. "Hey, what are you shaking for? Come on in and calm down." He opened the screen door. "Here, take a seat."

Dan went over and sat down facing the man. "Now just relax for a minute," the man said. "Then you can tell me why you are here."

As the man said that, something happened to Dan. He felt strong inside and began to speak fluently, talking to the man about Jesus Christ. It was like he was standing off watching himself. Scripture verses began to pour out as he shared what Jesus Christ meant to him.

Finally the Texan spoke. "You fellows have something real. I'm glad you shared it with me today."

Dan went down the street afterward, more excited than he had felt in a long time. It was really neat. Now he could hardly wait to get to Nassau and spend the whole summer doing this.

But the first day in the Bahamas, he got nervous again. Loren Cunningham was giving an orientation talk to the kids. At one point he said, "We will be dividing you up into teams of four to six for the summer. Don't expect to be put on a team with a friend or relative. In fact, we will make a determined effort to separate you."

A groan went though the group. Dan looked over at his buddies. They didn't like the idea either. But Cunningham went right on. "There's a reason for this. Friendships are usually formed around the common interests of people, like sports or work. Our interest will be in winning people to Christ. When you are with a group of strangers, you are more open to new ideas and don't react to relationships in a prescribed way. So there is more freedom for personal growth. In our case, we hope it is spiritual growth."

All the rest of the day Dan steeled himself for the announcement of teams. When it finally came, he was dumbfounded. They put Dan and Nick together on a team! The rest of the team were his buddies from San Francisco. And the leader of the group was Paul Bruton!

Then Paul came over to them with more news. They would be the roving team for the summer. They would go to an area for one or two weeks, then come back to Nassau and go out in a different direction, wherever there was a special kind of need to be met.

The guys laughed and pounded each other as they met together. It was going to be a neat summer.

IV

The first assignment for the team, Paul told them, was to get to Sandy Point, a little village on Abaco Island. "According to Loren," he said, "we'll have to fly to some offshore island and then take a boat across to Abaco to get to the town." The team grinned with excitement.

Dan could hardly wait. His first flight was just days ago when they flew over here from Miami. Now he was going up again. He began to feel a little different about it when they got to the airport and saw that they were going in a light plane. The boys stood around waiting to find out about their plane. They watched a plane circle the field. It came in, touched the runway, and took off again. "I wonder what he's doing," said Dan.

After a while, the plane landed and the pilot came over. "Are you the Youth With A Mission team going to Sandy Point?" he asked.

"Yes," they chorused.

"Well, I'm to be your pilot," he smiled.

The team fell silent. Finally someone got up enough nerve and said, "What was all that landing and taking off for?"

"Oh, that," he laughed. "I'm a jet pilot and haven't flown a light plane since I've been piloting jets. I thought I'd better practice before taking you guys up."

Dan didn't get scared, though, because the man explained he was going to fly the luggage and equipment plane. The team was to go in another single engine plane. So the boys set to work, quickly loading up his plane with all their suitcases, food supply, literature boxes, and a public address system.

They got it all in and walked eagerly over to the other plane. This pilot looked at them and said, "I can take only four of you."

The team stood still. Paul Bruton looked over at the other plane. "There's no room in it, either," he said. "Unless it was someone small we could cram into the corner by the door . . ."

Dan didn't move. He could feel every eye on him. "Okay," he said, managing a grin. "See you later." And he walked over to the other plane.

The trip wasn't bad, once they got up. But only too soon it was time to come back down. Dan could see the island below him and the team getting out of the other plane. It was the pilot who was hesitant now. "That runway looks in bad shape from here," he said. "Well, I guess we can give it a try."

The plane circled once. Then slowly it headed toward the ground, Dan's heartbeat rising in direct proportion. They came on in, Dan straining inside, trying to make the wheels touch down. Suddenly the engine started straining again and the plane rose up in the air as they roared by the rest of the team standing there, waiting.

The pilot circled the landing strip again. Once more he steered the plane down, and Dan could see the ground coming toward him. There was a rough thump as the wheels hit, but this time they stayed down. As soon as the plane stopped, Dan opened the door and got out. The rest of the guys came running over. "You should have seen your face," they howled. "You came zipping by us here and all we could see was this white face in the window with eyes nearly popping out!"

Dan grinned and started unloading the plane, hoping it would cover up the fact that his legs were still shaking. When they finished unloading, the team stood together and watched the planes leave. "We'll be back for you in two weeks," one of the pilots yelled before he took off.

Dan looked around. There was a little boathouse down by the water. All the rest was sandy beach and palm trees in the distance. The only sign of life was a large Negro woman, shuffling toward them on legs swollen and distorted with elephantiasis. She told them that there were only two other people on the island—the caretaker, Hezekiah, and his assistant.

"The skiff was riding four inches out of the water."

When Dan saw Hezekiah, he decided he was about the meanest-looking man he had ever seen. He just wouldn't smile at anything. He stared at them while Paul explained that they needed to get over to Sandy Point. Then Paul went on to say that if they didn't go today, they would need some sort of shelter tonight.

Hezekiah pointed to the boathouse. "You can stay there," he said.

The team moved in, glad at first for the shelter. But their enthusiasm didn't last. There were sand fleas everywhere. All night long they buzzed in Dan's ears. He lay there on his air mattress, covering his head with a sheet until it was so hot he couldn't stand it. Off came the sheet and back came the fleas. He tried to sleep, but when he opened his eyes and looked at the window, Hezekiah was there, staring.

By morning, Dan was ready to swim to Abaco if necessary. Everyone was up and packed within minutes. They went out to talk to Hezekiah, assuming he would take them across to Sandy Point in his boat.

"No," he said, shaking his head and pointing to the water. A squall had come up, and he wasn't going to venture out in it.

After a while, his assistant came by. When he heard their plight, he said, "I have a boat. You are men of God. If you wanted to, you could pray and still the waters so that we could make it over there."

Everyone looked at each other. That was a tall order. Finally Nick said, "If we don't get to Sandy Point we'll have to spend another night here."

That settled it. "Okay," said Paul to the man. "Get your boat and we'll start to pray."

The boys got the luggage and supplies ready, and soon the boat appeared. It was an eleven-foot skiff with a little motor. The boys looked at each other again, then began to silently load it with their supplies. With each addition, the boat sank a little lower. One by one the team climbed in. Finally the last one got inside. The skiff was riding four inches out of the water.

The man put it in gear. Dan looked back at Hezekiah standing on the beach, still shaking his head. Paul began to pray out loud and everyone joined in. They were still in the cove and the water was already rough. They began to come around the rocks which jutted out at the end of the cove. The open sea lay ahead. Suddenly, the water went smooth, like a giant hand pressed it down. The earnest praying stopped and Paul said, "Thank you, Lord," quite loudly.

When they saw Sandy Point's little dock ahead, the caretaker's assistant spoke. "This is faster than I have ever come over here before."

He was the first person out of the boat when they tied up. Running over to some people nearby he pointed to the team. "See these men," he said. "They prayed and God stilled the waters so that we could come over here." Then he disappeared on up the street, telling the story to everyone he met.

The team held services during the evenings and went door-to-door during the day until they covered the entire village with the Gospel. Everyone knew about them even before they came to a house. And they were all eager to hear what these "men of God" had to say.

Shortly after the team arrived, a young man named Napoleon came up to them. "I am a Christian," he smiled. "For five years I have prayed that my friends will come to Jesus. Now you pray with me."

The team began to make friends with these fellows. Before the two weeks were up, over twenty of them gave their lives to Christ. Every day the fishermen of the town would go out. Often they stopped at main towns on various islands in the Bahamian chain. They must have told the story of these "men of God who stilled the waters" everywhere because all the rest of the summer, wherever the team went, the people already knew about them.

Dan couldn't get over how neat it was, living on faith like this and witnessing to people. It was the most exciting thing he had ever done and he didn't want it to come to an end. By the end of the summer, when the teams came together again in Nassau, he spent a lot of time praying. He felt in his heart that he wanted to spend his life working like this, but he figured a person needed something special from God to confirm it. He prayed and prayed, but nothing happened.

So when he started back home, a deep frustration enveloped him. What could he do with his life? Well, he didn't know so he guessed the best thing to do was to go home and get a job.

Everything was different when he got back. His family had moved during the summer and now lived in a new home outside of San Francisco. All the familiar neighborhood was gone. He couldn't slip away to Golden Gate Park just by walking down the street. There were no sudden glimpses of the towers on Golden Gate Bridge as he rounded a corner. His friends were all involved in jobs or away at college.

He got a job in a sheet metal shop. His days fell into a predictable routine. Drive to work, drive home, eat dinner, and then watch television. This year he didn't have any responsibilities in the church youth group so there was nothing to tie him down and keep him busy.

Then one day, Jonathan came back to town. Dan was glad to see him. "This is my chance to help him," he decided when he learned he would be around for a while. "Come on over anytime," Dan said. "Maybe we can take off together on the weekends. Go skiing and stuff like that."

Jonathan grinned. "Good!"

And Dan determined to make every effort to bring him back to the Lord. Sometimes it meant being gone from church, but Dan excused it by pointing out the many chances he would have to talk to Jonathan. They skied together, cruised around town together, went to amusement parks together. And then they drank together.

One night Dan dropped in on the Sunday evening service at church. Afterward, when he got back home, Dan realized that he had walked into a church service drunk. A deep shame came over him. He began to contrast his life with the life he had lived last summer. Finally he knelt down. "Dear God, I've really gone back on my walk with You," he said. "Please forgive me. Help me to live an overcoming life."

He got off his knees and looked around the room until he found his Bible. The next morning he read it again before going to work. He began attending church again on Sundays and during the week. And he knew that he could not run around with Preacher anymore.

In the fall, Dan enrolled in Bethany Bible College in Santa Cruz, California. He still didn't know what God's call was in his life, but he knew he must learn all he could about following God.

Bible college was neat. He was busy all the time. There were classes all morning; then he worked in the afternoon. At night he was studying or attending a church service. And always, there were Christian kids around to fellowship with.

He'd go home sometimes on the weekends. More and more he found himself slipping over to Grandfather Illyi's house to talk. He would sit and visit with him, getting him to tell some of his experiences in leaving Russia. It seemed to give Dan the strength he needed to trust God for things when he heard how Grandpa had done it.

In 1920, a Russian minister, John Varonaeff, received the experience of the Baptism in the Holy Spirit while he pastored a church in New York City. He returned to Russia to tell of his new Baptism. Many people began to receive it. Grandfather Illyi was one of them. A minor revival began to sweep through the Ukraine with people turning to God. A new movement was born, The Christians of Evangelical Faith. Grandfather Illyi became an ordained minister. It was just during the time that the new Russian government was closing down the Orthodox churches.

Grandpa told Dan about the time in 1928 when he was led by the Holy Spirit to leave his home in the Ukraine, taking his wife and daughter with him. They traveled east as far as Uralsk where they lived for several years. During this time he started a church among the Cossack people.

One of Grandpa's brothers came on over to Canada and wrote to him in Uralsk. One night as Grandfather was beginning to eat supper, he felt a strong impression to go and get his brother's letters and burn them. He waited a moment. The impression came again, this time stronger than ever. He got up, took the letters from their hiding place, and threw them into the fireplace.

Then he went back and sat down to continue eating. A knock sounded at the door. When he opened it, Communist soldiers strode into the room. "We know you receive mail from America," they said. "We will find it and prove you are spying against the government."

The soldiers brushed past him and ransacked the home, taking anything which struck their fancy. All the while, Grandpa stood there with his wife and daughter by his side, while the fire slowly died in the hearth and the ashes turned black.

Dan marveled at the courage of this man—how he could be trying to escape the country because the Holy Spirit directed him to, and yet openly preach and start churches wherever he went, knowing it would mean imprisonment and possible death.

All the way across Russia to the Chinese border, everywhere Grandfather Illyi went, he spoke of Jesus Christ and usually ended up in jail. At one place they told him they were sending him to Arkhangelsk, a prison camp just below the Arctic Circle; yet he and his family were able to leave the city and continue their journey eastward. Each time the Holy Spirit would intervene in a miraculous way to guide and direct them.

Grandpa came very close to missing his goal when he got to the town of Sarkent right near the border of China. He continued to preach the Gospel and four people there found the Lord in a short time. He was imprisoned again, this time for two months. When he was released, the officials told him that he must return to Alma-Ata in four days, time as Russian officials there wanted to talk to him.

But Alma-Ata was back west, where they just came from. That wasn't good. Grandfather went home and told his wife and daughter the news. They began to pray. Once again the Holy Spirit gave him direction through prophecy.

"Today a man from China will come to you and ask whether you want to go to China. You will say, 'Yes, we want to.'"

That afternoon a man came to the house. He looked at Grandpa and said, "Do you want to go to China?"

That night, as soon as it was dark, they set out. It was forty miles to the border. All night the four walked. Just before dawn, they stopped and made a cover for themselves out of brush so that the border patrol couldn't see them. They sat in the intense heat of the desert all the next day, not daring to move. When darkness came at last, they stood up and began to walk again. Suddenly Grandfather Illyi collapsed. His whole body turned blue, and he was gasping for air.

The guide turned to his wife and daughter, his face set. "Leave him now; he is dying. If you are ever to get across alive, you must come with me now."

Dan's grandmother shook her head. Praying aloud, she and his mother picked up Grandfather the best they could and began carrying and dragging him toward the border. When the guide saw that they wouldn't be put off, he came back to help. Suddenly, the blue color disappeared from Grandfather's face and his breathing returned to normal. He stood on his feet and walked with them to safety.

"Wow," thought Dan as he looked at his grandfather. God had led his family and friends on a fantastic journey and kept them safe, all because they were willing to listen to His voice and trust Him for every need.

When the spring came, Loren Cunningham returned to Glad Tidings for a service. Dan sat and listened, while Loren described how teams would work in Jamaica and Central America that summer. Dan's mind went back to the previous summer. He didn't want to spend another summer like that again in his life. Then he remembered the Bahamas the year before. He was really happy then. But college was costing a lot. How could he go on Summer of Service, knowing he had to pay for school in the fall? The memory of Grandfather Illyi's story came to him. If God could lead Grandpa, couldn't He lead him too? Okay, he decided. He would step out on faith and make preparation for SOS in Jamaica. Then God could open or shut the door, whichever was best.

After church a lady came up to him. "Are you interested in going on Youth With A Mission this summer?" she asked.

"Yes," he said.

"My house is for sale. I'll have an offering for you when it sells," she said.

A smile rose up from deep inside him. God was really

helping him. By the time he left church that night, he had received several job offers for work after college was out.

When he came home the first of June, he was really excited. He began following up on the job offers. Every single one had fallen through. In desperation he decided to go see the lady who promised him the offering. Her house hadn't sold.

Dan came back home and went to his room. What was God trying to do to him? Here he had told all of his friends he was going, and really stepped out on faith. He fell to his knees and poured out his frustration to God. After a while, he stopped and idly picked up a book on the bedstand. It fell open to a story where a child was asked by her mother about what she was doing.

"Oh, I was helping God," the little girl answered.

"Just what were you doing?" the mother queried.

"I was opening up the flowers for Him."

Dan closed the book. The words had jumped out at him with insight into his actions all day long.

"Okay, God," he prayed. "First I want to thank You for all that You have already done for me in the past. And now I want You to know that once again I'm going to trust You for every single need in my life."

Within days he was flying to El Paso, Texas, for the Kickoff Crusade, with enough money in his pocket to pay his fare on SOS. After he had prayed that day, jobs opened up and people came up to him with money, telling him that the Lord had spoken to them about his need, even though Dan hadn't mentioned it to anyone.

VI

It was a long and busy summer. Dan's team worked in Jamaica, and then in August, they were able to fly to the Caymen Islands to work. When he returned to college he felt renewed in his spirit. He determined to dedicate every vacation period to some kind of outreach ministry. Sometimes it was a YWAM Domestic Crusade. Other times he worked on Indian reservations or took mission trips to Mexico.

The next summer he went to northeastern Oregon where

he logged during the week and ministered in churches on Sundays. The following summer he worked as a counselor in church youth camps. During each winter he trusted God for his financial obligations and saw Him provide through part-time jobs, scholarships, and anonymous gifts.

One day near the end of his junior year, he got some sad news from home. Jonathan was dead. Dan walked in a dark cloud for days. His buddy and friend was gone. They never were able to help the one who needed it in their relationship. He remembered the time Jonathan came home after a tour of duty in the marines. He had tried to start a new life but his drinking was such a problem that he couldn't hold a job. He joined the army and was shipped to Germany. From there he went to Vietnam where he died.

It was Jonathan who used to talk by the hour of returning to Russia someday. Ever since they were kids he had talked that way. Jonathan was the one who made the high grades. Jonathan was the one named Preacher.

One night Dan was back at his home church. Pastor Thomas was preaching. In the course of the sermon he remarked how wonderful it was that people were able to escape from Communist countries. Then he said, "But it is disappointing to me that everyone is coming away, and no one is trying to get back into these countries with the Gospel."

The words haunted Dan as he went to class and hung over him when he knelt to pray. He remembered coming home on the bus from Jamaica. It was then that a special desire had broken forth inside him and he wanted to go to Europe. Somehow he felt that he could minister there. But how, or when?

One day he talked with Loren Cunningham about it. "Why don't you just step out on faith, Dan?" Loren said. "If you know this is what God wants you to do, then make your plans. He'll send in the finances."

Dan came home that summer and told his folks that he planned to go to Europe. But even as he said it, it seemed strange; for he had no clear way of doing it.

Now as he prayed, the desire to go was still there. But there still were no answers. He committed his way to the Lord again and waited, returning to Bethany for his senior year.

One night he went to a service where YWAM Caribbean Area Director, Floyd McClung, was speaking. They were talking afterward when Floyd looked at him. "Dan, why don't you go to Russia? You know the language and everything," he said. "You could have a real ministry there."

Dan looked at him with a start. "I've been thinking a lot about something like that. I don't see how I could go, but I'd sure like to do it."

"Why don't you just go?" Floyd said. "God can meet your needs if this is His will. Loren has started a School of Evangelism in Europe. They have people come in and speak to the students. People who have special ministries like literature evangelism or personal soul winning—things like that. Loren says that they're going to have a man called Brother Andrew speak for a week this year. He has a ministry of taking Bibles into Communist countries."

Now Dan began to pray earnestly about his move. One night after a missionary service at the college chapel, he stayed and prayed for a long time. A great peace came over him as he prayed. He had an assurance that he was to go to Europe. He got off his knees and walked to the back of the chapel. Some of his friends were there.

"Guess what," he said. "I'm going to Europe next year."

They all looked at him rather stunned. The next day he found an envelope in his school mail. Inside was a slip of paper with his name misspelled and five twenty-dollar bills. Dan stood holding them for a moment. To him they represented the first of the money that he would need for the trip. But his school bill kept coming before him.

"All right, God," he said in his heart. "I'll make a covenant with You. If You help me pay off my school bill by graduation, I'll take it as the seal on my trip." With that he walked over to the business office and applied the money to his bill.

Now everything started to fall into place. He could leave the United States in June and meet a YWAM team in Europe and work on Summer of Service there. Then he could come back to the School of Evangelism in Switzerland and spend the fall in language study. In the spring they would have the evangelism seminars. Then, after that . . . No. He wouldn't think about it or make plans. Every time he thought about it, a deep desire to return to Russia would sweep over him.

By the time he walked down the aisle at graduation, Dan had received and earned enough money to pay off his college bill completely. He didn't have any money left over, that was sure, but God had met the need. He left the campus that day with the assurance that God had called him and that he was walking the right path.

But then the next morning when he woke up at home, he realized he had only three weeks in which to come up with the money to get to Europe and pay the tuition and board for the time he was in School of Evangelism. He sat down and figured up what he needed. Twenty-one hundred dollars!

A whole week went by. Not a cent came in. Nor were there any job opportunities. Wednesday was the last day he could pick up his plane ticket. He didn't know for certain how much it was, but he figured it would be over three hundred dollars. That weekend, a church sent him an offering for fifty dollars. On top of it, he received one hundred dollars from a family. Then another one hundred dollars came in. The day he went to buy his ticket, another family sent him one hundred dollars. He walked into the travel agency with the money in his pocket. The woman wrote down the cost of a flight to New York. Then she added the flight to Luxembourg. "That will be three hundred fifty dollars," she said.

Now there were just a few days left. Dan drove up to Oregon to minister in some of the churches where he had worked two years before. He had a good time of preaching and sharing what God had done in his life. But he never made any appeal for funds even though the need seemed overwhelming to him.

After the services, a number of people came up to him saying that God had impressed them to help on his trip; then they slipped an offering into his hand. Sometimes they were teen-agers who stood there shyly while they dug deep into their pockets and pulled out fifty cents.

Dan drove back to California, awed at the goodness of God, both in meeting his needs and in the way He had used people to do it. None of the people who gave him money were well-off financially. It was like they were all part of one body, giving and receiving to meet each other's needs. It was the neatest thing that he had ever seen.

He had just one week left now to sell his 1965-model car. It sold within days bringing a good price which helped considerably on the large amount he still needed.

One night he sat down and added up the money. "All I need now is a couple of hundred!" he realized. But where would it come from? It felt like he was walking on a ledge as he tried to calmly go about packing and getting ready for his flight. The day before he was to leave, the money still hadn't come in, and he started to get panicky. Once again he tried to commit it to God.

That night his folks sold a piece of property they had been trying to sell for years. Their eyes were shining as they handed Dan the amount he needed to complete his covenant.

Dan climbed on the plane the next morning and waved good-bye to his family and some friends. Maybe by the time he saw them again he would have met their relatives and friends in Russia.

As the city of San Francisco faded away below him, Dan's mind went back to the family gathering a few nights before. Grandfather Illyi was sitting alone and motioned for him to come over.

Dan went and sat down beside him. Grandfather leaned over and spoke quietly. "Dan, before I ever left Russia, God spoke to me one day. I have never told anyone this but He gave me the promise that His work was not finished there and that once again He would move by His Spirit in our land. When I came to America, I always thought that God was keeping me safe so that I could return and bring the message of the Gospel of Jesus Christ once again to my people. But now I am seventy years old. I cannot go. So I give you the mantle of this promise. Will you carry it for me?"

TWO ANTI-FANATICS

The first day on Youth With A Mission nearly finished off Linda McCullough and Joanne Thomasson. "These people are all wet!" Linda spouted to Joanne when they met back at church before the evening service. "I just can't take it, Joanne. This is it." She went on, her dark eyes flashing. "I feel like a hypocrite or something at the door."

"I know just what you mean," Joanne answered. "It just isn't right doing this."

"I've always been against this type of evangelism," Linda grumbled. "It's geared to put a person on the spot. I just can't go along with it."

Before they could talk further, the service began inside. "Well," sighed Linda. "I guess we'd better go inside until we think of something constructive to do."

The two went in and sat down. The young people began to sing choruses but Linda sat still. Her mind was going back over the events of the last few weeks. What had happened? Up until today she was positive that she was to go on Youth With A Mission's Summer Of Service. But now she was having real second thoughts about spending her summer this way.

She thought back to the night when she first heard about YWAM. She was talking to Del Hutchinson at a party in Fresno, California. He was telling her about his experiences in Africa on YWAM's one-year Vocational Volunteer program.

"Hey," Linda said. "That sounds more like what I'm looking for. My folks want to send me to Spain for a graduation present. But I'd like something like this where I could live with the people and experience the country firsthand. Besides, there would be a real purpose to the trip, not just sight-seeing."

When Linda told Joanne about it later, she was just as excited. Her folks were giving her a trip too, as a present for college graduation. But the moment the two decided to go with YWAM and sent in their applications, everything started working against them. Friendships became strained with many people in their lives, over unrelated problems. It got so bad, that after graduation the girls took off for a couple of weeks to the mountains where they spent a lot of time praying and seeking after God.

Both of them came back convinced that this was indeed where they were to work during the summer. So they continued to prepare for the trip. Linda was relieved when they finally started off in her brand new sports car. She assumed that now their troubles were behind them. But the trip turned into a seven-day fiasco with car trouble plaguing them all the way from their home in Madera, California, to Galveston, Texas.

Each day a new gas station attendant in a new town had a new answer for what was making the warning light on the dash come on. And each new attendant charged them a fortune to replace it. But the warning light continued to burn. They left the car with Linda's relatives in Dallas and flew on down to Galveston. They were just beginning to relax when they had to go out and face strange people at the doors. It really got to Linda when some of the people slammed the door right in her face.

"I've never had people so rude to me in my life," she fumed now as she thought about it.

Her mind snapped back to attention as Loren Cunningham began to speak. He was the one who got them sold on YWAM in the first place. When she and Joanne heard him speak in Fresno, he seemed real to them, not phony, so they figured the program must be pretty good.

Now Loren caught her attention. All the while he spoke, she could feel a sense of conviction rising up within her. Then Loren invited everyone to come forward and pray. Linda went down, half-mad and half-yearning to talk to God, and find out some answers.

She found a corner and knelt down. Her frustration boiled up again and she began to talk it out with God. After she quieted down, in her mind's eye she could see the Lord. He was reaching down to take her up to Him.

Now her common sense started in. "Well, Linda," she thought. "You're not going to live through the summer. God must be showing you that something is going to happen to you."

"No, God," she retorted. "I don't want to die."

The presence of the Lord began to grow in reality to her. It was like Jesus Christ was standing right there and asking her to give up, to really, really give up her life to Him. Up to now she always thought that this sort of thing happened only to fanatics and missionaries and people like that. But right now it seemed perfectly normal and natural, not spooky at all.

"Okay, Lord. If you want to take my life, then fine. You're gonna hurt Mom and Dad but if You want to go ahead, then okay. If this summer is to be my last effort for You, I'll do it."

Then she waited. But nothing happened. No thunderbolts from heaven, and worse—no assurance that she would live.

She really didn't know if anything at all happened until the next morning when a door was slammed in her face as she began to tell a woman about Jesus Christ. Now, instead of anger, a deep hurt welled up inside. She wanted to pound on the door and beg the woman to just listen to the fact that Jesus loved her. That He alone was the answer to the problems in her life.

The rest of the week was just great for Joanne, too. Later, as they bounced along in the school bus that YWAM leased for the summer, Joanne shared her reactions to the week with Linda.

"I think my moment came the night Loren preached on commitment to doing God's will," she said. "That night I had to say, 'God, I don't care what my will is or what I want to do. I just want Your will.' "

"I know just what you mean," answered Linda. "I think this is really going to be a great summer in Central America."

It took the bus four days and nights of travel to get to Mexico City. Somewhere along the way, Linda wrote a letter home. She had been gone only three weeks now, but already she missed the comforts of home, like eggs and bacon for breakfast with lots of coffee.

"Warning!" she wrote. "When I get back home, don't let me see peanut butter, tea, powdered milk, or canned meals. But good news, Mom! I'm eating everything, no matter what color or how it tastes."

She smiled as she thought about it. It was really true. Kind of a schizo feeling of love and hate at the same time. Really wild. "Here all our water has to be filtered. Also, we can't go without shoes because of hookworms."

She paused a moment, looking out the window at the fields of giant cacti and the purple mountains in the distance. "You know, all these things sound horrible until you're in it. And I'm sure the things I'll write this summer will probably sound bad. But it really won't be, so don't get discouraged. It sounds worse than it really is . . ."

The road got rough for a while so she stopped a minute. "It's weird," she began again. "I miss all of you tremendously. But if I had the opportunity, I wouldn't return yet. Oh well, maybe I can explain the feeling when I get home," she finished.

II

The bus broke down in Mexico City. They had to send to the United States for a part. The leaders assured the teams that there was no problem. They planned to have them spend the time witnessing to the students on the campus of the University of Mexico.

"Wow," Linda mouthed silently across the room to a smiling Joanne. But the next morning as they set out to face their first Spanish-speaking people, both of them were feeling a little scared. It was the real thing, now.

Linda walked across the campus with Cliff Anderson and Joy Dewey. They came up to a young man in the Medical Plaza. The three began to talk informally with him. At first he didn't seem interested. But other students began to gather around him, listening to every word. The three kept on talking about their experience with Jesus Christ. Soon there was a group of twenty-five students listening and asking questions.

"It was fantastic!" She smiled as she told Joanne about it

later. "Those kids are really hungry to hear about Jesus Christ."

"I know," Joanne nodded, sharing her day's experiences.

Later that night, part of the group was sent on to Guatemala in a smaller vehicle because of obligations for services there. Linda was chosen to be part of the group.

So it was several days before the two girls got together again, this time in Guatemala City. "You should have been with us when we crossed the border," Joanne said as soon as she got off the bus. "It was really neat. You remember that bridge made out of planks where you cross from the Mexican border station to the one in Guatemala?"

"Yes," Linda said.

"They wouldn't let the bus go over it. They sent it around another way but we had to walk across the bridge. Then when we got to the other side, we had to wait for several hours for the bus to make it.

"We didn't have anything to do so we began to sing choruses. A man came over and listened. Later we found out he was the president of this little border town. He invited us to come over to his house and sing and talk with his wife. We went and sang for them awhile, then prayed for his sick children who were running high fevers. Then the man and woman said they wanted to accept Christ!"

"That's wild," said Linda. "What would have happened if you didn't have to wait there?"

"I know," smiled Joanne. "It's taking me a long time to learn this, but I'm seeing where if we're open to God, he can turn our disadvantages into His advantages. That's probably the big lesson that we'll have to learn over and over again this summer."

After working in Guatemala, the groups traveled on to Managua, Nicaragua, to work in that country for the rest of the summer. They got a good night's sleep and everyone had a chance at a real shower again. Then they divided up all the summer's supply of literature and food to each team. The following morning, one by one the teams set out to their first destinations. It was the first time the whole group was divided so the good-bye's were a little sad. A strong camaraderie had developed among the group during their experiences traveling and witnessing.

The team Linda was on set out for the city of Leon, north of Managua. Their chief goal was the university campus there. The kids went out and witnessed to students on the campus during the day, then participated in services in local churches at night. Some days they also went door-to-door in the barrios around the city.

One day the team was asked to participate in a water baptismal service. Early in the morning a pickup truck, already filled with people, came rattling up. The kids climbed in, greeting the local Christians. On the way out to the village, the truck broke down. Some of the men started to work on the motor. Linda watched as the rest of the folks got out of the truck and calmly went over to a banana tree and sat down in the shade. Someone got out a guitar, and the group began to sing choruses. Linda remembered the panic she went through every time something went wrong with her own car.

The group finally made it to the river. Afterward, the newly baptized Christians invited everyone to come to their little home and hold a service. It was getting late when the group finally piled into the truck to start back to Leon. Linda was so hungry she wanted to scream. The truck started down the dirt road. Then a tropical rainstorm hit. Sheets of rain poured down. There was no protection for anyone, so they started singing and clapping their hands to keep warm. Finally they got back to their quarters and everyone dashed for the food box.

"How about this?" called Linda, holding up a big can of chili beans.

"Yeah!" the team cried and started lighting the little stove. Someone else made a big pot of hot chocolate with powdered milk. Dressed in dry clothes at last, the kids sat around eating the hot food and talking over the adventures of the day.

Shortly after that, one of the Area Directors came up from Managua to see how the team was getting along. He was talking to Linda a few minutes. "You'll be rather surprised when you see Joanne and her team when we meet next Saturday in Managua," he said. "Everyone on the team has been pretty sick for two weeks now. They've all lost quite a bit of weight."

But Linda was still shocked when she saw Joanne on Saturday. "You're so thin that when you smile, all I can see is your teeth and two, huge blue eyes!" Linda cried.

"Oh, come on," Joanne wailed. "Is it really that bad?"

"Well, what did they decide you guys have?" asked Linda.

Joanne lowered her voice. "Look, you're not supposed to spread this around or everyone will get excited. The doctor said we had a mild case of typhoid."

"Wow," said Linda slowly. "How come?"

"When we first left Managua, we were in this little suburb. One night we went to eat at this man's house. I know, that's one of our rules, never eat where we can't be sure of the water or food. But he was so nice and we felt we could witness to him.

"Then it really hit when we moved out to a little village down near Costa Rica. We were working in this tiny church. No kidding, the sanctuary had a thatched roof and dirt floor and was smaller than my bedroom at home," Joanne laughed. "Anyway, here we were with everyone sick at his stomach and having diarrhea."

"Oh, brother," sighed Linda.

"It was really funny some of the time. They brought Jimmy Woodhall down to join our team about then, so he wasn't sick. He would always be saying something funny so here we were, just weak and sick and then laughing. He called it the 'Big D' because we all thought it was dysentery. But anyway, the doctor gave us all some pills and we're feeling a lot better."

"But you had typhoid shots, didn't you?" Linda asked.

"Sure, we all did. No one could figure out how we got it. They said we had the distinction of being the sickest team ever on YWAM. The doctor said it's so common here that when people get it, it's like getting a bad cold in the States."

Linda hooted. "A bad cold! Listen. If your folks could see you right now, you'd be put on the first plane home."

"I know," Joanne said seriously. "But they don't know about it. You know, it's really amazing what you can do if you want to. Here we were out in this little town. But as soon as any two of us started feeling better, we'd go out and do some witnessing. It was great because the people were

"We could hear the volcano, and the sky was filled with ashes."

open and hungry for the Gospel message."

The two fell silent a moment. Then Joanne said, "Look, you haven't told me anything about Leon. What happened?"

"We had some really good results," said Linda. "Both at the university and in the barrios. And they made me a team captain. Oh, and we held some high school assemblies in the town we were in last week, Chinandega. They turned out good, too."

"We had a school service. And wouldn't you know, the teacher of the class where I spoke was an atheist," laughed Joanne. "But the Lord really gave us wisdom. The man told us to just talk about the United States. So we did. Then in the middle, he raised his hand and asked why we thought Christ was the answer to life! It was really neat."

"So far this summer has really been wild," observed Linda.

"Oh, yes, and you know when the volcano erupted in Costa Rica last week?" Joanne said. "We could hear it, and the sky was filled with ashes and stuff. They put us on an alert in case we had to be evacuated.

"And Linda. You wouldn't believe the pastor of that tiny church where we were. In the church service at night, he played a jawbone of a cow for music!"

"Oh, come on, Jo," Linda laughed.

"No, really. It had some of those little metal disks on it, like you see on a tambourine. He would hit it in time to the music and rub a nail on it. It really sounded pretty good."

All too soon the day was over and the kids set out once again for new destinations. Linda's team was assigned to an area in the back country. One night, several days later, she stood stirring the food for supper, cooking in a big pot over the open fire. Her mind went back to all the times she cooked this way just for fun on camping trips. Now it was for real, like washing clothes on rocks in the stream and bathing by turning a gourd full of water over herself.

Later that night she stood at the back of a crowd, watching the Y-wammers conduct their final service for the town. There was only one Christian family when the team came to town, so the kids held the services in their front yard. It was a good crowd that night. Linda could tell that nearly the whole town was there. She stood quietly, trying to record everything in her mind so she wouldn't forget it, for the summer was nearly over.

The only light was a kerosene lantern strung on a wire between two trees. A cloud of flying insects were banging into it and pigs were walking around through the crowd. The sky was filled with stars hanging so low she felt she could reach them. Someone was preaching in Spanish. It was so dark she couldn't see who it was.

In that moment, Linda understood what being a missionary was about. It was being able to stand there, listening to people talk in a language that wasn't her native tongue, smelling the aroma of a crowd who lived where there was no running water and at the same time, having her mind bombarded with thoughts of clean clothes from a dryer and cold water from a faucet. Yet through it all, wanting one thing above all else, that these people would understand that Jesus Christ was their personal Savior. That He wasn't just a crucifix on a wall, but that He was alive now and waiting for their hearts to turn to Him.

"Okay, God," Linda said in her heart. "If You want me to stay here for the rest of my life, I'm willing."

A feeling of warmth and security enveloped her like she never knew before in her Christian experience.

III

Linda and Joanne rode in the bus with the rest of the Y-wammers as far back as Mexico City. Then they flew to Dallas to get Linda's car. As they climbed aboard the plane, it seemed like they were entering another world. The stewardesses were so perfectly groomed. Linda and Joanne suddenly remembered that there were such things as beauty parlors and dress shops. The carpeting on the floor looked luxurious after weeks of dirt floors and adobe walls. The girls sat down and Linda reached up and turned on the air conditioning.

It seemed like the plane barely took off before the stewardess served them dinner. Linda and Joanne looked down at their trays. "Wow," they giggled together. It was worth two months just for the delight of this moment. When they finally finished eating, they put their seats back and began to share their summer.

"I remember one day when the impact of what we were doing really hit me," mused Joanne. "We were talking to this lady who really wanted to give her life to Christ. But she knew she couldn't do it and continue her common-law relationship with a man who was married to someone else. Finally I said to her, 'You know, it's got to be all or nothing when you serve Jesus Christ. You can't serve Him halfway.'

"Linda, after that my words began to haunt me. It was like God was saying them back to me. What right did I have to go and spend my summer telling people this if I wasn't willing to spend the rest of my life living by those very same words."

"I know exactly," said Linda. "I don't know what we can do or how we can do it. But I mustn't go back to what I was before. If my testimony is to mean anything to these people, I must live exactly as I've told them to live, even if I never see them again."

The trip back to Madera was like a rerun of the trip down in June. Car trouble all the way. As they drove along, their talk turned more often to the future.

"I'll be so glad to get home," sighed Joanne.

"Me, too," laughed Linda. "But I already know that once I say 'Hi' to everybody, I'll be ready to go again."

"Yeah, Madera's too small. We've seen too much of the world now. I just couldn't be content in a little town again."

"Hey!" cried Linda, a gleam in her eyes. "Maybe we could move up north. Someplace like San Francisco. You know, far enough away from the family to be independent, yet we could drive down on weekends sometimes. Maybe God would open up some door for a fantastic ministry there that we could do while we worked."

"Wouldn't that be neat?" smiled Joanne.

As soon as they got home, several churches wanted to have them come and tell about their summer. They were to speak in Linda's church first on Friday night. Joanne was glad she didn't have to talk much that night. She was starting to feel bad again, like she did in Nicaragua.

She went to the service and sat and listened. Afterward she came up, eyes shining. "Linda. You know what hit me during the service? What would happen if young people went door-to-door in Fresno? Couldn't we see the same results that we saw all summer long?"

Linda looked at her a moment.

"Sunday night we're supposed to speak at my home church in Fresno," Joanne went on. "I could talk to the pastor then and see if he's interested. We could head it up since we've had training on YWAM."

"I think this is something *you* should do, Joanne," Linda finally said. "I'll wait and see what God has for me."

Joanne shrugged and smiled.

By Sunday night she hadn't been able to keep food down for three days. "It's probably just the excitement of getting back home and all," she told Linda on their way to church.

When they got there, Joanne went in to talk to the pastor while Linda waited. Within minutes she came out grinning mischievously. "You'd better come in and talk. I included you in all the plans and the pastor wants to finalize plans now so he can announce a door-to-door witnessing crusade in the evening service."

Linda laughed in spite of herself.

The next morning Joanne went to the doctor. He took a lot of tests and promised to let her know as soon as he had something definite to report. He phoned that afternoon. "Get down to the hospital at once. It's hepatitis."

They met her at the hospital with a wheelchair covered with a sheet. She rode to her room in an elevator marked "Quarantine" and they picked her up by the corners of the sheet to put her in bed.

"There are no drugs that can help you," the doctor said. "The only cure now is complete rest. We'll watch your blood count. It will have to go way down before you are well. You'll probably be this way for at least a month."

Linda came to visit her. Joanne couldn't help laughing when she saw her. All she could see was Linda's brown eyes. There was a cap on her hair, mask over her mouth and nose, and she was wearing a long gown with long sleeves.

"When you drag me into something, you really do a good job," Linda sighed as she sat down. "They want to go ahead with the witnessing crusade in Fresno. So they've talked me into running it solo."

Joanne laughed. "I'll promise to pray for you, how's that?"

The crusade went off as scheduled, starting that very week. Linda brought Joanne reports each day. A good group of the church young people turned out and several Saturdays were spent going door-to-door in the city.

Joanne was able to come home in about seven weeks. The doctor told her she could go out a little. Her first venture was to the final Saturday of witnessing in Fresno. The day before, the doctor took another blood count, promising to call her as soon as he got the results. If the count was really down, it meant she could get into the swing of things again.

Joanne returned from Fresno to find her mother waiting for her. "The doctor phoned," she said quietly. "He says your blood count is still up. You are to go back to bed for another month."

Joanne turned and walked to her room, flopping down on the bed. She couldn't hold back the tears. Another whole month of this! When was she ever going to get away to the new life she dreamed about in San Francisco?

The doctor told her that he thought she contracted the hepatitis during her original sickness in Nicaragua. "All of this for one drink of unfiltered water," she thought now. How come? It just didn't seem fair for God to allow this to happen to her.

As she lay there with her face buried in the pillow, her mind went back to the moment in Galveston when she made her commitment to God. The words of her prayer came back to her. "I don't care what my will is or what I want to do, God. I just want Your will." She was willing to say it when she faced the new adventure of a strange land. But now it seemed like God was asking her if she was willing to say it here at home.

She lay still a moment. She couldn't see any purpose for it all, but she decided to accept it in blind obedience. "All right, God," she prayed. "Here, too."

IV

A moment later, Linda came bouncing into the room.

Joanne knew without asking that her mom must have phoned and told her right away. Linda had a gleam in her eyes again.

"You know, Joanne it's really been fantastic having this door-to-door witnessing in Fresno," she said.

Joanne nodded absently.

"Well," she went on. "What would happen if we tried to do something like it here in Madera? If we had a dedicated group of kids, we could cover this whole town with a witness of Jesus Christ."

Joanne looked at her friend a moment. So that was the answer! "Here it was, right under my nose," she thought, "and I didn't see it because my sights were set so far away."

She grinned. "Okay, but what can I do to help?"

"You can sit right there in bed and I'll get a portable typewriter and fix it up on a bed table. Then you can start writing letters to every pastor in town, telling them of our plans."

Soon the girls had drafted a letter of introduction. Then they both set to work typing up more than fifty letters. In the letter they described the program and said they would be calling for appointments to talk with them personally about the outreach.

At first, most of the pastors were a little apprehensive. Madera was a conservative town. They had never tried an unusual program like this before. One pastor couldn't help registering his surprise when he saw them.

"You just don't look like missionary ladies setting out to conquer a town," he laughed. "I've never seen missionaries driving sports cars before!"

But the pastors weren't against it. They saw the possibilities of what young people could do by witnessing in their own town. And soon nearly every church contacted decided to join the outreach. There were Presbyterians, Baptists, Methodists, Episcopalians, and Pentecostals. A Spanish-speaking church with a large group of young people wanted to take part. The ministerial association had the girls speak to them at a meeting and promised their support. Then the local Christian Businessmen's Club offered to help by paying part of the cost of tracts, advertisements, and printing supplies.

Saturday, December 7th, was set as the kickoff day. Linda

and Joanne got ready to go to the Presbyterian church where the kids were to meet. Behind them were weeks of exhausting work. They named the program VIVET! Latin for "He Lives!" They put together a training manual from their YWAM materials and mimeographed it. They held services for recruitment in many churches. In the process, they developed a core of workers. One of them was an artist who drew up a design of the name, VIVET! and they mimeographed it on stationery and literature.

The girls decided that they would keep the program going for one month, figuring the kids wouldn't stay interested in it any longer. They set up prayer meetings every Thursday night. Saturdays would be spent in witnessing and training.

Saturday morning Linda stood up in front of the group. There were about twenty-five teen-agers in front of her. Some of the pastors were sitting in the back to hear what she had to say. She plunged in. She had spoken about three sentences when a kid raised his hand.

"Yes?" she smiled.

"What do you mean when you say a 'born-again experience'?"

"How many of you don't know what I'm talking about?" Linda asked. Several hands went up. "Wow," thought Linda. "What a challenge! Here we are training kids to go out and win the world and some of them haven't met Christ themselves!"

Linda chose her words carefully. "These kids are going to take in everything I say and they're gonna watch the way I live," she thought. "I'm not a student anymore; I'm a teacher now." She looked over at Joanne and could tell by the look on her face that she was realizing the same thing.

They took the kids out to the areas that they had chosen for the first day of witnessing. The kids were scared to death, but each one got out of the car with a brave smile. Then Linda and Joanne started praying like crazy.

Later, when the young people returned, they were all excited and yet still scared at the same time. "We kept meeting our friends from school," they said. "They didn't know until today that we were Christians. Now we have to live by what we said."

The girls smiled. They knew exactly what the kids were talking about.

"Do you have any tracts for teen-agers?" asked one. "I'd like to give them to my friends at school on Monday."

At the end of the month, the kids wanted to keep VIVET! going. They continued to have prayer meetings and a witnessing program until spring. Then the group began to lay groundwork for a Youth With A Mission outreach in the Central Valley of California during the summer.

Linda and Joanne continued in another ministry. This one came about as a result of the witnessing program. The young people on the team came to a new place of commitment in their lives so they phoned the girls constantly to get help on each new step in following Christ. Some of the most dramatic conversions in town were not door-to-door but in the lives of school friends. Linda and Joanne helped guide these new converts, or advise the young person who was doing follow-up work with them.

Often the girls' phone rang in the middle of the night. It would be one of their VIVET! kids reporting that a friend had gotten too high on drugs or was in some other trouble and asking the girls to pray. And the girls prayed.

Linda got a job teaching English as a second language at Fresno City College. Joanne became a social worker in Madera, then met and married Joe Brazil the next fall.

The lives of the two girls are quiet and somewhat ordinary, except when God sends someone across their path who needs help spiritually. But they have come to consider this ordinary too—a daily living out of Christ's life as they go about their routines and duties. To them that isn't being fanatic at all.

CHINESE AGITATOR

A hurricane was moving up through the Caribbean. It pushed a ball of hot, humid air in front of it which now hung over the city of Nassau, Bahamas. Most of the young people were too excited to really notice the heat. They had just returned from various outlying islands in the Bahamian chain where they had spent the summer evangelizing. All day long they talked of their adventures, telling stories of conversions and amazing miracles.

But to David, the heat was oppressive. It seemed to bear down on him, causing whatever was frustrating him to increase in intensity. He knew it wasn't the stories of the other teams on Youth With A Mission. For his team saw good results from their work, too.

"What is it?" he thought. He felt incomplete. Like a huge disappointment inside. The teams were going to work here in Nassau for two more weeks before returning to the United States. David realized he almost dreaded the two weeks; yet at the same time he didn't especially want to return home yet. Something wasn't finished.

David looked at his watch. There was still over an hour until the evening service started. "I think I'll go pray awhile," he thought. "Maybe I can find some answers."

He came into the youth hall and went up to the front altar. Kneeling down, he tried to quiet all his thoughts. It seemed to get hotter and hotter. The large fan whirred, trying to circulate the heavy air.

Deep inside him, a quiet voice spoke. "What about the Chinese people here in Nassau. Who is going to minister to them?"

"The Chinese?" David thought, almost stunned. In his mind he saw the streets that he walked during the summer. He knew that there were thousands of Chinese living throughout the Caribbean. Many of them had fled China but were not able to get into the United States. They settled where they could, all over the world.

David's dark head bent very low now over the altar rail. "The Chinese?" he asked again.

Then he began to see some scenes from the last few years of his life. He remembered the day he learned that he was named "Mr. Christ's Ambassador—USA" by his denomination, and the excitement he felt at placing top in the nation in a contest based on outstanding character, Christian service, and scholastic achievement.

Then his mind went back to the time five years ago when he saw a vision. It was just a fleeting picture in his mind, but he never forgot it, taking it as the call of God. First there was a picture of a huge wall. Then there was a scene of lots of houses, close together. Finally he saw a Chinese coolie straining as he pulled a rickshaw.

After that vision David began preparing his life for the ministry. He got into the outreach activities of his church right away. They said he was too young to teach Sunday School so he joined the group who held services in the jail. Through the years he worked as a leader in youth groups, both in the church and on the high school campus.

In the back of his mind he figured that he'd probably be a missionary someday. But that was a long way off; the door to China was closed.

Now his mind jumped to another moment back in his hometown in California. The people of the little Chinese church came to him one day and asked him to help them in their church. He went downtown and talked to his pastor.

"I feel they're pressuring me," he said. "I was born and raised here in Bakersfield. I'm more American than I am Chinese."

Now the words hung over David. He realized that he could achieve every status possible to an American, that he could talk and live like an American, but nothing could ever erase his ancestry from his face. He was and always would be clearly and irrevocably Chinese.

David understood what God was asking him. "So this is it," he thought. "The moment I put way off into the future has come now, even though I'm only eighteen."

It made sense. There wasn't anyone else on the teams who could do this job. He knew how Chinese would react to a message brought by a white man.

"But if one of their own comes," he thought, "one who has been raised in a Chinese home, one who understands the intricate customs, one who can talk a little in their language . . . what would happen then?"

Still, he wasn't sure. "Lord, I'm here for only two weeks," he prayed. "It really won't be valuable unless I have something to leave in their hands. I'm willing to go, but it seems a waste of time without literature . . ."

And leaving that for God to think over, he rose from his knees and went to the back, pushing open the door into the hall. The local pastor and Loren Cunningham were just coming in the front of the church. The man stopped when he saw David.

"Say," he said. "We have a whole lot of tracts written in Chinese here at the church. Would you have any use for them?"

So the next day, David started a new approach to YWAM's personal evangelism. Instead of going door-to-door on special streets, he and his partner went from restaurant to restaurant and store to store, looking for Chinese faces. The initial contact with a Chinese would then bring invitations for the boys to visit the whole family at the apartment above the store or in a nearby house.

There was a new excitement now as David went out each day. All the memories of his Chinese home, which he had tried to bury in his teens, came back to him. He was able to speak the language of the people. He remembered the many customs. And as he looked at the Chinese tracts in his hand, he became acutely aware that he was walking in a path that God had chosen for him. Up to now he had interpreted his vision as a call to a country. But God showed him that he could minister to a people wherever he was in the world.

II

A few weeks later, David returned to Bethany Bible College. He barely arrived on campus when he heard about a little Chinese mission in Watsonville, several miles away. They needed a pastor. He didn't have to struggle to make the decision this time.

On the weekends David would go over to Watsonville and work with the tiny group.

Later on in the fall, David met Lula Baird. She and her husband were returned missionaries from the Orient. They had begun a work in Chinatown, San Francisco.

"We call it the Chinese Christian Center," she told David. "It's located just one block from the commercial section of Chinatown. We've had it open only since March, but there are many converts already.

"And that's what I want to talk to you about," she went on. "Most of these are young teen-agers, just thirteen and fourteen years old. It's the most remarkable thing, but invariably, they are the ones who are reached in our services."

David smiled.

"What I want to know is," Lula said, "could you come up and minister to these young people during Christmas vacation? I feel they need to hear a young preacher, someone they can identify with."

"I'd like that very much," said David, for he always enjoyed working with young people, maybe because he was still a teen-ager himself.

Several weeks later, David came through the narrow streets of Chinatown to his first service. For the first time, Chinatown didn't seem like another world to him. The brightly lit stores were filled with Chinese imports. The smell of Chinese food cooking hung in the air. Every once in a while he would catch a glimpse through an open door into the dark little sweatshops. Here Chinese women labored all day long, sewing garments for manufacturing companies.

The Christian Center was housed in an old storefront building. David walked in and found a lounge instead of a sanctuary. It was because there was more room in the basement, someone explained, pointing to some stairs. David went down the stairs carefully, and then stood and looked around the room.

It was a basement all right, with damp cement floors. The

"For the first time, Chinatown didn't seem like another world to him."

only air that came into the room was through a grate which opened onto the sidewalk. David could hear the footsteps of people as they walked on the street above. The ceiling of the room was filled with plumbing and other pipes. The chairs were unmatched, donated from other churches.

Suddenly young people began clattering down the steps. The stark lines of the room seemed to fade as each new group came into the hall. David looked over the audience. Most of them were teen-agers, born and raised in this inner city of San Francisco. He knew that there were even some who would go home that night and watch their parents burn incense and pray to idols. Yet these young people had been uniquely touched by God. It really was unusual, David thought. But he had no answers for the phenomenon so he began to concentrate on his sermon.

It seemed like any other sermon to him. But as soon as he finished, the kids crowded around the little pulpit. They began asking him questions faster than he could answer. They wanted to find out as much as they could concerning spiritual matters. Their eagerness amazed David.

As he stood there, looking at them, a quiet assurance came over him. He knew somehow that his ministry here wasn't finished, it was only beginning.

When he finally left the Center that night, there was a peace within him that he couldn't explain. He knew that he would be back here ministering. This was where God wanted him. A few months later when the Bairds asked him to come and serve as assistant pastor after graduation, his answer was ready.

David was chosen to be the class speaker at Bethany's graduation. For days he spent his free time walking among the redwood trees on a quiet part of the campus. He was thinking and praying about what he was to say. He walked a rugged path one day. The dark, sweet smell of damp earth hung in the air. He looked up at the redwoods towering above him. They seemed so strong, able to withstand the centuries . . . A phrase came to him, "Calvary Road."

"Yes," he thought. "That's a perfect picture of what my life has been and what I've learned these past years. If I could sum up all my ambitions, it would be my desire to follow

Christ." He decided he would share this life theme with the thousands of people in the audience.

When the warm May day came, David stood up before the crowd. "Christ's task was to reconcile a depraved world unto God," he preached, his face taut with intensity. "His only concern was to do the will of the Father.

"Observe the way Christ walked the Calvary Road, for the Calvary Road is the Christian life."

The sermon was the keynote of his own spiritual life. Looking out at the hundreds of faces before him David cried, "The field is the world. The cost is self!"

A few days later he stood speaking to the kids at the Center. The glamor was gone, but he was just as excited as at graduation. For now he had the chance to put into practice all that he preached.

He plunged into the work in San Francisco with enthusiasm. He preached at the English-speaking services. The young people usually attended these. The older Chinese who still spoke their native tongue attended the Chinese-speaking services conducted during other hours. The young people's group continued growing with remarkable speed.

Just one year after he began working in San Francisco, he was installed as the pastor of the English section of the work. But the more he ministered in Chinatown, the more he became aware of his lack of fluency in speaking Chinese. Now he was paying the price for all the years he refused to learn Chinese at home because he was an "American."

One day in August, Mr. Baird passed away. A few days later Lula came to David.

"The full burden of this work is too much for me now," she said, "for there is also the Chinese outreach in Oakland."

David nodded, sensing what was coming.

"The Center here in San Francisco needs one pastor," she went on. "One who can devote all his time and energy to it. With your American/Chinese background and Bible college training, you seem perfectly equipped for this ministry."

David felt excitement rising up inside, but he held back. Now he saw that his lack of language was a real barrier to an effective ministry.

As if she knew his thoughts, Lula spoke. "Your biggest

problem right now is language. You need at least a year in Hong Kong to study Cantonese."

David looked up. "But what about the work here?"

"I'll try to run both the outreaches," she said, "but I can't do it for long. If you are to go; you should do it as soon as possible."

"Let me pray about it," David said quietly.

Long into the night David waited before God. "What about the young people here at the Center?" he asked. "This is a crucial time for them."

As the nearness of Christ came over him, he saw that the longer he put off language study, the more he would be involved in the ministry of the Center. It would never get any easier to go; it would always be difficult.

"All right, Father," he prayed. "I will make plans to go. Please guide my steps for I want this year away from home to be a fruitful one . . ."

III

When the plane landed in Hong Kong the next spring, David tried to keep calm, but there was an excitement inside him that he could hardly contain. Here he was at last, as close as he could get to China.

His last year of work in San Francisco prepared him for life in Hong Kong. It was like a huge Chinatown, only when he came to the edge of the city, San Francisco wasn't surrounding him. There was just more of China.

The streets were thronged with masses every day. There were old vendors in dark garb sitting beside their wares on the sidewalks. Passing them were the prosperous businessmen in western dress. When the schools let out, the streets would fill with thousands of bright-faced children, laughing as they went to their homes.

Everything that David saw seemed to be Chinese. Everything he read was Chinese too, for he was concentrating on his language study. Everything he ate was Chinese, and he found that nothing could have made him happier. And through it all was a growing burden for China and the Chinese. The great spiritual needs of the humanity packed into Hong Kong seemed almost to crush him at times.

He was invited to teach English to the Chinese students in a Bible school. He accepted readily, glad for the chance to be of help. The first day of his English class, David got on the train to travel out to the school located outside of town. It wasn't until he was seated inside, packed in together with the rest of the third-class passengers, that he realized this same train would eventually end up in Canton.

"Inside!" he thought. "Some of these people right here beside me will ride up to the border and pass on through. Today in just a few hours they'll be inside China."

His stop came and he climbed out. Then he stood as the train pulled away, watching it disappear toward the border. Someday, maybe someday . . .

At the Bible school he learned more about China. Communism wiped out not only the organized Christian church but all the pagan religions as well. Maoist teachings had replaced religion. The language was simplified by the Communists so that millions of formerly illiterate Chinese could read and write.

"What will happen to this spiritual vacuum when Mao dies?" David wondered.

The students told him about thirteen young people who had attended the school. When their training was over, they felt called of God to go into Communist China to share what they had learned, even though it meant certain death. So they slipped across the border. Only two of them had ever been heard from again.

It was a long time before David went to sleep that night. The day ran through his mind like a wild movie. But the memory that kept coming back was the moment when he was on the train. He felt that huge land of his calling was a giant magnet, pulling him closer and closer.

From then on, each Wednesday, what started out almost as a lark for David became a nightmare. Every time he boarded the train for the Bible school, the pulling inside began. He sat on the hard seats of the third-class coach, looking out the window and trying to ignore the Chinese around him. But the closer he got to his stop, the worse the pulling became, until a deep burden for his land engulfed his whole being.

Still he would sit, looking out the window. He was a Chinese now, and Chinese do not show their feelings. Not a muscle moved in his face, but inside he was crying out loud in agony, "Just a little farther. Oh God, if I could go just a little farther . . ."

His time for language study came to a close all too soon. He was due back in San Francisco to be installed as pastor on Easter Sunday morning. There was just enough time left for a brief side trip through Southeast Asia. He wanted to see the work being done among the Chinese who lived in these countries.

Everywhere he ministered in Asia, Pakistan, and India, he found Chinese. And everywhere he saw the same problem. Pastors were overworked, trying to fill three and four positions at once in little Chinese-speaking churches. Other Chinese communities had no church at all. Everywhere David went, he saw a place where he could stay and do a work. Many of the people felt the same way and would ask him to stay and work with them.

One night David could take it no longer. Over and over in his mind played the scenes of the past year: the faces of the scattered Chinese, begging him to help them; the faces of those at home in San Francisco confidently awaiting his return. Then the scene of that third-class rail car came crashing into his mind. The magnet started pulling again, and David felt his heart being torn out of him.

"Oh God, I'm not enough. I'm not enough!" he cried out.

At that moment, God spoke to David's heart. The answer was so simple and so perfect that he was astounded that it hadn't occurred to him sooner. The faces of the teen-agers in San Francisco came before him once again as the Lord spoke.

"Multiply," He said to David's heart.

Waves of understanding broke over David. That was why the unusual revival among the young people. Why, right now there were at least ninety Chinese kids capable of being trained for the ministry either at home or here! He already knew of five in the group who told him they felt called to return to the Orient. These were teen-agers who grew up in Chinese homes, who loved the diet of rice, who were Chinese in their thought patterns and customs. Teen-agers who had a whole life ahead of them to invest in God's work.

"All they need now is training," David thought. "I can take all I learned on YWAM and in Bible college and translate it into the oriental way of life."

Now he could see God's future for him. Yes, he would come back here in a few years to spend his life. But when he returned he would come back with a band of young people, yes, even an army if God so chose. They could work all over Southeast Asia. And then, when the door to China opened again . . .

IV

Thirteen months after he left California, David was installed as the pastor of the Chinese Christian Center in San Francisco. He began setting up programs of internship and training immediately. The young people took over the Friday night youth service so they could receive training in all phases of church leadership. They were responsible for visitation. They planned and conducted periodic outreaches, going door-to-door in Chinese sections of the city. They began Chinese churches in other areas of high Chinese populations.

In the fall of 1969, they were able to purchase an old fish market near Fisherman's Wharf. In their spare time they began to hammer it into a new Center for the growing work. By May of 1970 they were able to hold the first service in it.

David's preaching still centers around the Calvary Road. He says things like, "Our lives are not just to follow Jesus' teachings but to live Jesus' life and follow Him up Calvary. That's Christianity!"

But this is only half the story. David has a brother. Stephen spent a year in Manila, Philippines, on the Youth With A Mission Vocational Volunteer program. He did personal evangelism in the many dormitories which house the hundreds of thousands of students at the universities of Manila. Stephen returned to California burdened with the need for more Chinese workers in the Orient. Stephen was asked to become pastor of the Chinese Christian church in Los Angeles. There Stephen found a remarkable thing. The majority of the congregation was young people. They were teen-agers who grew up in Chinese homes. Teen-agers who loved the diet of rice and Chinese food. Teen-agers who were Chinese in their thought patterns and customs. Teen-agers who had a whole life ahead of them to invest in God's work . . .

CONQUISTADOR

The first day of school was to remain forever fixed in the memory of Ruben Vargas. Much of what happened to him later in his life seemed to stem from that day. He was brought into the first-grade class and introduced to the teacher.

"Hello, Ruben," she said. "You go right over there and sit."

Ruben went over where she pointed and sat, not daring to move. School seemed like a different world to him. All he knew was his home and the building of the little Spanish-speaking church which his father pastored in San Jose, California.

Ruben looked around at the other children. The first thing he noticed was that he was bigger than any of them. The second thing he became aware of was that they all seemed to know what was happening and he didn't.

The bell rang for recess. All the kids got up and went outside, so Ruben followed silently. He watched them play until another bell rang. They all started back to the building. Ruben looked around for someone to follow. He couldn't remember anyone's face. No one was familiar. He wandered into the building. There were doors and hallways everywhere, stretching ahead in a strange maze. He didn't know where to go.

Slowly he walked down a hallway, looking at each door. Finally he reached the other end where doors opened to the street. Ruben slipped outside. He knew where things were out here. Home was down the street this way.

He was home just a short time before a school official came looking for him. "What happened?" asked the man.

Ruben didn't know what to say. He was afraid to talk to this official man.

"Well, you belong in school. Come along back with me and

I'll take you to class."

Obediently Ruben went back with the man. They walked into the first-grade classroom and he took Ruben up to the teacher. Ruben looked into her face. It seemed to him that she was very angry. She began to reprimand him for leaving school. Ruben stood there, her words crashing down on his head. It was the harshest scolding he had ever received.

"Now," the teacher finished, "go take your seat."

Ruben looked around. He must find a chair and sit down where no one could see him. It seemed like he didn't belong here, like everyone was in on a secret except him. Then he saw an empty chair. He hurried over to it and sat down, wishing he could melt into the wood.

A child spoke out. "Hey, you can't sit there. That's the teacher's seat!"

Amid giggles and stares, Ruben got up again and began to look for another empty place. He felt caged, like he was being beaten into a corner.

The feeling was to return over and over again as he grew up. Anytime he was called on to speak in class or stand up in front of a group, he would feel cornered and would be unable to perform. He was always fatter and taller than anyone else his age so he became extremely shy, seeking every means possible to stay inconspicuous.

One day when he was thirteen, he was playing outside the house with his brothers and sisters. He and one of his sisters got into an argument.

"No," he yelled at her as she ran inside and locked the door. "You let me in!" he called, hitting the door with his fist. Then he turned to the new window beside the door which his dad put in last week. Calling to his sister inside, he started knocking on the glass. Suddenly, it shattered.

All Ruben could see at that moment was what his father's face would look like when he found out. It meant that Dad would punish him. Ruben turned and ran from the house. Halfway up the street he looked around. His father was coming out of the house after him.

Ruben forgot that he weighed over two hundred pounds, and he began to run faster and faster, dodging traffic as he ran from one street to another. Finally he slipped to the side of a building and stopped, panting with exhaustion and fright. Slowly he peered around the corner. His father was nowhere in sight.

"Oh, boy, that was a close one," he thought.

Slowly he walked back out into the sunshine and headed toward downtown San Jose. Downtown was his favorite place. He used to sell papers there in the afternoon, to help out with the finances at home. No one ever looked at him downtown. Even when they bought a paper they didn't seem to really see him. So every afternoon he'd walk the streets screaming the headlines, pretending that he was an invisible man.

Now as Ruben walked along, the old invisible feeling returned. He began to relax. He wandered through a couple of stores. Then he went to his favorite place, the television store. When he sold papers, he had stood there fascinated for hours. There was even the night when he had come home and handed his mother two pennies saying, "That's all I could sell today."

In fact, it was television that caused Ruben to drop out of church. The stores started staying open on Thursday evening, which was the midweek-service night. Telling his folks that he could sell more papers at night, Ruben went downtown to watch the evening shows until the stores closed.

Today Ruben returned to his old haunt and stood for hours while the shows changed on the television sets. Finally he realized it was getting dark and he was hungry. He turned away from the shop and started home. Then he remembered. That nameless fear welled up inside him again. All he could think about was the punishment that waited for him. He shivered in the cool night air and began walking. He knew he couldn't go home; he was afraid. He walked and walked, wondering what to do. It was quite late when he happened upon a used-car lot. The cars looked cozy and safe. He slipped inside the lot and began to check the car doors. He found one that was unlocked so he climbed in the back seat, locked all the doors, and settled down to sleep.

Ruben lived this way for several days. Then one day the family found him. "Why didn't you come home?" they asked. "Why did you run away?"

Ruben looked down at them. He wanted to say, "I was afraid. Please don't punish me. I was afraid." But he couldn't because he was still afraid.

Ruben continued to run away. Every little upset now would send him away from home. Sometimes he would go to his aunt's house and stay there. He didn't know that she called his folks so they wouldn't worry. One time he didn't show up anywhere. Early one morning his mother lay in bed, praying for his safety. Just then she remembered how the children told her once that Ruben slept in cars. She got up and searched the car lots until she found him.

Another time his father saw him in a store downtown. But Ruben saw him coming and slipped away in the crowd.

After one of these episodes, Ruben was settling down back at home and his father came to him.

"Ruben, I want you to go for a ride with me in the car," he said.

The two climbed in and drove off. As they rode along his father spoke. "Ruben, what do you think about me?"

Ruben looked over at his father. He really wanted to know how he felt about him! Ruben relaxed. He felt free inside, like he needed to get this out. Slowly he began to tell his father about the punishments and his fear of them.

His father listened. Then he said, "Son, I am the pastor of a church. The people look to me for an example. If I do not raise my children to be good, then how can I preach to the people?"

Ruben hadn't thought of it that way before. As his father continued to talk, Ruben felt like cords that had bound him were being cut away. When the two got back home, they climbed out of the car and went inside. Ruben settled down in the living room with the rest of the family. He wasn't afraid of his father anymore.

II

From that day on, Ruben never ran away from home again. Now home was his refuge from the rest of the world. When he left junior high and entered the tenth grade, the kids seemed to explode around him. They did what they pleased;

they had minds of their own. Again Ruben didn't fit in.

One day he stood outside the high school stadium, peering through the fence at the football rally. The school principal was speaking. Suddenly the principal looked toward the fence. "Everybody should be inside the stadium taking part. No one is to be outside the stands . . ."

Ruben turned and hurried away. He couldn't go in. He just didn't belong there. He had nothing to say when he was with a group of young people. It was like he was all locked up inside and no one had the right key.

Not long after that, Ruben stayed home from school one day. He messed around the house awhile, enjoying the chance to escape from his problems. The next morning when his brothers and sisters got ready for school, once again Ruben decided to stay home.

After several days, his brother, Abraham, was worried. "Look, Ruben, you can't just stay away from school. I've talked to the principal about you and he wants you to come and talk to him."

"Oh, no," said Ruben quickly, his dark eyes growing large. Now they wanted him to talk to the principal. What would he say to him? The nameless fear came again, and for days, all Ruben could worry about was what the principal might do to him if he returned. So Ruben became an official high school dropout in the tenth grade.

After a few weeks, a man in the church came up to Ruben. "Did you know there was a job opening at Spivey's restaurant?" he said.

Ruben's eyes lit up with interest. He was getting bored hanging around doing nothing all the time. "What for?" he asked.

"Dishwasher. Why don't you take it?"

"Oh, I couldn't," Ruben started in. The man must have sensed his fear for he held up his hand.

"We can recommend you to the manager; that way you won't have to be interviewed."

Ruben thought for a moment. Now he remembered that quite a few people from his dad's church worked there in the kitchen. "I'll know everybody," he thought, "and they'll help me if I don't understand."

"Okay," he said. "Okay. I would like that."

The first day he was really nervous. But when he got to the restaurant and saw that he really did know a lot of the people working there, he relaxed a little. His friends showed him how to run the dishwasher. By the end of the day he was doing it smoothly and confidently.

And at the end of the week, when he saw his first paycheck, he was even happier. For the first time in his life, he had money of his own to spend.

Ruben enjoyed the job. He was busy and at ease among people he knew. In his free time he looked for ways to help the others in their work. He liked it when they commended him on the good job he was doing or thanked him for helping them. He especially enjoyed helping the cooks, so he continued to gain weight.

One night when he got home, his folks were talking excitedly. Evangelist Oral Roberts was coming to San Jose for a giant tent meeting.

"Oh, boy!" thought Ruben. He had seen Oral Roberts a lot on television and listened to him on the radio. He always liked to hear the preachers on the radio. Often he sat and listened to his radio until late at night, just to hear the men preach. His father was his favorite preacher, and before Ruben quit going to church, the preaching was the part of the service he enjoyed the most.

"Imagine hearing this great man in person!" Ruben thought. "I will go and see him."

Ruben got to the tent one evening just before the service started. He walked around the back until he finally saw an empty seat on a corner aisle. He went over quickly and sat down. A minute later, a man walked up.

"I'm sorry," the man smiled, "but this is an usher's chair. You can't sit here. Come with me. I have another seat for you."

Why did he always have to find the wrong chair? he wondered as he got up to follow the man. They started down the aisle and when Ruben finally realized that the man was taking him near the front, it was too late to turn back. With the smile of a person offering Ruben the whole world, the usher gestured to a chair right in the front row. Ruben sat down, afraid even to lift his head and look about him.

Finally he got up the courage to glance around. There were television cameras everywhere and now one was pointed right at him. Ruben ducked down again, wishing he wasn't so big.

It came time for Roberts to preach. He stood up and began talking about cowards—who is a coward and what makes a person a coward.

"He knows I'm here!" Ruben thought in amazement. It was as if Roberts was up there revealing every secret of his life. He finished preaching and began to invite those who wanted to accept Jesus Christ to come forward. Ruben stood there wanting to go, but too afraid to do it in front of all these people.

He slipped out with the crowd when the meeting was over. From that night on, something was different inside him, like something which hadn't worked for a long time was beginning to move.

After work one night, this something was working again. He decided to walk home instead of taking the bus. The moon was out and the streets were quiet as he walked toward home. The sermon Oral Roberts had preached came back to him now. It kept going over and over in his mind. An intense longing swept over him and he prayed for the first time in years.

"Dear God. I know I'm a sinner," he said as he walked along. "I want You to do something with me. I don't know what I could ever do for You ... just look at me. I'm too fat and I'm shy. And God, I'm afraid. But if You could, God, would You use me?"

III

The next Sunday afternoon Ruben went to the Roberts meeting again. His father went with him. They got there late and the place was packed. They stood outside watching through the door flap. Roberts was just finishing his sermon and giving the altar call.

Ruben's father looked up at him. "Wouldn't you like to have a ministry like this some day?"

Ruben heard it but he couldn't take time to answer. He

was too busy trying to get up enough courage to walk down the aisle. He knew this was the time to publicly commit his life to God. Maybe if he said it out loud he could do it.

"I'm going forward," he said to his father.

Then he turned back to face the long aisle. His courage was gone. In a minute he would be too terrified to move. He tried putting his foot forward. When he did, something inside got started moving and he was able to put the other foot down. Then he was walking into the aisle with a group of people. Quickly he slipped into the middle so that people couldn't see him as they walked up to the front.

He stood between people at the front. Then Roberts announced that everyone was to go to the prayer tent outside at the back. That meant walking back up the aisles past the people again. Ruben slipped out a side exit.

Ruben began attending his father's church again. He took part in the services and began to serve God in his daily life.

In February, an evangelist held meetings at the church. As Ruben sat and listened to the man preach one night, he knew in his heart that he wanted to be a preacher more than anything in the world. But he didn't know how to start.

After the service he sat talking to the evangelist. "How did you begin to be a preacher?" he asked.

"I went to Bible school," the man answered. "That's where I learned how."

Ruben thought about it a minute. "Well, how do you go to Bible school?"

The evangelist laughed. "I'd better talk to your father about you," he said and left the room. Ruben's father came in a few minutes later.

"I have telephoned the Latin American Bible School in La Puente," he said. "You can go right now. The new semester is just beginning."

"Wait, wait," said Ruben now. "I don't have money or anything. I will go in September."

That June another evangelist came to San Jose. He held meetings in the San Jose Prayer Garden. The Latin American Pentecostal churches of the area were the sponsors. The meetings centered around help for those who were seeking the Baptism of the Holy Spirit.

Ruben decided that if he was to ever become a preacher, he would have to receive this experience. Maybe that would give him the power to overcome his shyness and do something for God.

One evening before the meetings began, Ruben's father came to him. "They are asking the sons of the different pastors to be ushers during the meetings."

"Oh, no," Ruben said, backing away. "I can't do that. I can't stand up in front of all those people."

"Ruben, you are the son of a minister," his father said. "And you are enrolled in Bible school to become a preacher. Everyone knows it. You cannot let your family down now."

"Okay," Ruben sighed. "But please can you put me in a corner somewhere?"

They put him at the back of the balcony. So all he had to do was point to empty seats instead of walking down in front of people.

Every night when the man finished preaching, he gave a call for those who wanted the Baptism in the Holy Spirit to come forward where he could pray for them. Ruben would take off his usher armband and put it in his pocket. Then he went down to the front with the rest of the people.

The first night the evangelist had the people line up in front and he went down the line putting his hands on their heads and praying for them. Ruben slipped around to the side and knelt by some benches where no one would see him. He had seen a lot of people receive the Baptism in the Holy Spirit. Sometimes they really got excited about it. He wanted the Lord to give it to him nicely and quietly here in this dark corner.

It didn't work. So the next night he went forward again, moving a little closer to the center of the crowd at the front. By the third night he was close enough for the evangelist to lay hands on him. As soon as the man finished praying, Ruben dropped to his knees as he continued praying so that no one could see him in the crowd of people.

On the tenth night, Ruben really felt like he had faith to receive. By the time the evangelist got to him in the line, Ruben was already thanking the Lord because he knew he was going to receive the Baptism. Tears were streaming down his face and within moments after the evangelist prayed for him, he was speaking in an unknown tongue and glorifying God.

The next Sunday he stood at his usual place in the back of the balcony during the afternoon service. Someone asked for Ruben Vargas to come to the platform. Ruben went down to the front.

"This is the son of Pastor Vargas," the speaker announced. "He has received the Baptism of the Holy Spirit this week. Please come and give your testimony."

Ruben mounted the platform and spoke fluently as he told of his new experience. It wasn't until he was back up in his usual spot that he realized he had been up in front of two thousand people and he hadn't even thought about being afraid. .

In September, Ruben boarded a bus for school in Southern California. This would be the farthest he had ever been from his family and home. But the students were friendly to him when he arrived and he forgot about his shyness as he helped fix up the simple buildings for the new school year.

One of the teachers pastored a Spanish-speaking church nearby. When Ruben wasn't traveling with the school choir, he would go with Rev. Camarillo and help in his church. Most of the time he helped by canvassing the town for Spanish-speaking people who were interested in attending the new church. Ruben liked that. It was fun knocking on doors and talking to people, even when he had to do it alone. He had something to talk about so he forgot about himself as he worked.

Near the end of his third year in school, his classmates began to ask Ruben his plans.

"What will you do when you get out of school?" they asked.

Ruben shrugged. "I don't know."

"Are you going to be a pastor?"

"No, I can't be a pastor. It takes too many sermons. And you have to stand up in front of people all the time."

"How about an evangelist?"

"No."

"Then what are you going to do?"

Ruben got embarrassed. He really didn't know. What *could* he do for God? he wondered.

Late one night he slipped over to the chapel to pray. He must find an answer for his life. After a while, Rev. Camarillo came in and prayed with him.

Finally Ruben looked up. "Brother, how can I start as a minister?" he asked. "All I can ever do is help. I like to help, but that's all I can do."

"Why not start there?" said Rev. Camarillo. "I know of a group of young people who go around and do door-to-door work something like you did with me in Pico Rivera. They're called Youth With A Mission. You always seemed to enjoy that kind of work."

Ruben wrote and got an application. Then he concentrated on trying to graduate. His grades weren't high enough in several classes. One day he went around to each teacher.

"What can I do to help my grade?" he asked.

Each one gave him the same answer: write up a paper on the subject they would give him so that he could show them how much he had learned. For three weeks after graduation he labored night and day writing out the reports he needed. By the end of June he had finished them and got his diploma as well as his first ministerial credentials.

He went home and packed his bag for Youth With A Mission. He planned to work on the Spanish-speaking team in the Dominican Republic. A friend of his was going too. He offered to take Ruben in the carload to Miami, Florida, to meet the rest of the team.

On the day he was to leave, Ruben got the news that his friend and another fellow were driving through a mountain pass on their way to San Jose, and the car had gone over a cliff. Both of them were in the hospital, one not expected to live. Slowly Ruben unpacked his suitcase.

IV

Ruben stayed in San Jose and helped his dad in their church which had now grown into a thriving work. He kept busy all year. He directed the young people's group and was assistant superintendent of the Sunday School. On Sunday nights he directed the service, and during the week he did visitation with his father.

In May he applied to go on Youth With A Mission again. This time he had no finances, but he made plans to go anyway. One day the phone rang. It was the YWAM office with the news that his way had been paid and he was to come.

Once again Ruben packed his bag. But then the realization hit him that he was going to be in a foreign country. He started getting scared. He remembered how Rev. Camarillo would fast and always had a breakthrough in his spiritual life when he did so.

"Okay," Ruben said. "That's what I'll do."

He began the first day he left home. He rode down to Southern California with a minister friend, Rev. Alex Bazan. Alex was serving as the director for the Latin American team that year.

As they drove along, Alex offered Ruben piece after piece of his wife's homemade cheesecake, unaware that Ruben was fasting. For the first time in his life, Ruben had to refuse food when he was desperately hungry. When Ruben finally explained to Rev. Bazan that he was fasting, Alex apologized and told him how to break the fast gently at the end.

Ruben went on the Spanish-speaking team to Mexico. When they found out that he was a Bible school graduate, they made him an evangelist for one of the teams. "You are to preach in the services, too," they said.

Ruben gulped, thinking of his sermon supply tucked away in his suitcase. He had exactly three.

"I tell you what," he said. "You have the other evangelist preach on the first night in each place and I will preach on the second." He was remembering that the teams planned to work only one week in each town.

It worked out fine except that by the end of the summer the young people on the teams were begging him to come up with a new sermon.

Ruben enjoyed the door-to-door work most of all. It never seemed hard for him to talk to people individually about God. One day, he and his partner knocked on a door. A tall man with a beard opened it and listened intently as Ruben explained the plan of Salvation. The man called to his wife. Then they both made a decision for Christ.

Later, someone in town told Ruben about the man. He was a professional wrestler. Ruben took a deep breath. "Oh?" he said, hoping no one could hear his heart pounding out loud.

Ruben really liked the work that summer. He almost hated to leave and come back to San Jose. But when he did, he immediately got some invitations to preach in Spanish-speaking churches. Now he *had* to get some more sermons. He got a big black book of sermons and began to read them. When he found a good one, he copied it carefully into his notebook.

One of the services was at a church in Hanford, California. After the service, a visiting pastor invited him to conduct a revival at his church in Arizona. Ruben was really excited as he got ready. This was his first real evangelistic campaign.

When Ruben got off the bus in the little town, he found a one-street town with a population of about five thousand people. That made Ruben relax a bit. The only thing that bothered him now was his sermon supply. He had enough to preach one every other night for two weeks. That gave him two days to work on preparing a new one. Even then, if it came down to the wire and the new sermon didn't look too good, Ruben knew he could use one from his supply.

Ruben spent each day praying and working on a sermon. It was hard work, for now he was writing them on his own instead of getting them out of a book.

When Ruben was on Summer Of Service he discovered that he really did have more power in his life when he fasted. So during these meetings he fasted during the day, eating only one meal after the evening service. At first, the discipline was hard. But it worked so he knew he must abide by it if he was to ever have a fruitful ministry. There were times when he would feel weak and the smell of food would be more than he could take. He would be ready to give in; then the question would come to his mind:

"If you cannot be an effective minister, what can you do?"

A picture of the dishwashing machine at Spivey's would come to him and he would have renewed determination to continue his fast.

A day or two after Ruben arrived in Arizona, he sat watching the pastor announce the special meetings over the church loudspeaker. The outside loudspeaker did an efficient job in the small town. The pastor was talking about the meetings and then he said, "If any of you are sick in body, come to these meetings. Rev. Vargas will pray for the healing of sick people."

"Oh, boy," Ruben thought. "Now what will I do? I've never prayed for anyone like that before!" Quickly he got up and left the room, looking for a place to pray.

That night he tried to act as if praying for the sick was something he did all the time. He called for those who wanted to be healed to come to the front. Then he went down the line and prayed for each one. Afterward a few people testified to being healed of ailments like headaches, and he was grateful for small favors.

That night he noticed a man sitting at the back. When the altar call was given, the man slipped out so Ruben didn't have a chance to talk with him. The next day as Ruben was praying at the church, the man's face kept coming before him. He felt he should try to reach this man some way. Just then the pastor came into the building. Ruben told him about the experience.

"What can I do about him?" Ruben finished.

"Oh, I know who he is," said the pastor. "I can take you to his house to see him."

They got in the car and drove out to the man's home beyond the town. It was a little one-room cabin. The door was locked and no one was home.

"Maybe my brother knows where he is," volunteered the pastor. "He works in town at a gas station."

The pastor's brother did know. "He came here today," he said. "He told me he wanted to die and that he was going to kill himself."

Now Ruben and the pastor set about in earnest to find the man. They looked all over town and finally returned to the cabin to check it one more time. The man was at home. As soon as he saw Ruben and the pastor, he began to weep.

"I have such agony," he said. "I'm so sick now, all the

time. The doctors tell me they can do nothing."

"What is your sickness?" Ruben asked.

"Cancer of the stomach."

Ruben felt impressed to talk to the man about Jesus Christ. "You know that Jesus Christ loves you so much that he died for your sins?"

"Yes," the man whispered.

"When you give your life to God, that means you are willing to serve Him," Ruben went on.

The men bowed their heads after a few moments and the man asked Christ to come into his life.

Then Ruben felt that they should pray that the man would be healed. Once again the men prayed. Ruben felt a burst of faith in his heart as he prayed for the man.

When they finished Ruben spoke. "Okay, brother, we will take you to the doctor now for an examination."

They packed the man into the car and drove back to town to the doctor. Ruben and the pastor waited and waited at the doctor's office. Finally the doctor emerged from the examination room.

"There is nothing wrong with this man," he said.

V

By the time the meetings came to a close, Ruben was invited to hold meetings at another church in a nearby town. And so it went for several months. Ruben spoke to little Spanish-speaking congregations in remote areas of Arizona. When he went to a place, he never asked for an offering. If they could give him one, he thanked God for meeting his needs. If not, then that was the way it was. Sometimes he would get only two or three dollars, but he knew that the congregation gave it in love, and it was enough to get him to the next town, so he thanked God for it.

After six months, he returned to California. Once again he made plans to go on Summer Of Service. The Spanish-speaking teams would work in Guatemala, Nicaragua, and Honduras that year. Ruben prayed and felt he should go.

"But you have no money," said his parents.

"I know," replied Ruben. "But if God wants me there, He

will provide the way."

Then he went to his room and packed his suitcase. He called the bus station to find out about a bus to El Paso, Texas, where the teams were meeting. He found that there was a strike on and nothing was running. Well, he had no money anyway, so there was no need to worry yet.

Several days went by. The weekend was coming and still nothing happened. He knew the teams were to leave El Paso on Monday morning for Central America. Then he got a call from Alex Bazan.

"Ruben!" he said. "I just got a call from the Youth With A Mission office. Someone has taken care of your expenses and you are to come this summer."

Before the evening was over, other money came in to pay for his bus fare to El Paso. He called his brother and asked him to drive him to the bus station. When they got there, the bus drivers had just gone off their strike. Ruben boarded the first bus for Texas.

He decided to fast again. Central America was something new and he was getting nervous again. When the young people got to Guatemala City, they began services in four churches that very night, even though they had been on the road a week without rest. As Ruben prayed for the sick that night, he was thankful once again that he fasted three days on the trip down. He could feel the anointing of God on his life, and he saw many people healed and others make decisions to serve Christ.

In midsummer, part of the young people's group went to Nicaragua. Ruben had to stay back in Tegucigalpa, Honduras, with some of the others because of passport problems. Ruben set out with the kids to find some way of ministering in this unexpected situation.

The team got permission to preach to some soldiers. The message of true Salvation so impressed the leaders listening, that they asked Ruben and the team to hold a series of daily meetings at the jail. There were about two thousand prisoners there, the kids discovered the next day. They sang and gave their testimonies and Ruben preached. A move of God began among the men and every day there were some who gave their lives to Christ. Visitors' day came and went at the jail.

Afterward the officials were amazed. No one got drunk this time or took drugs smuggled in by their families.

The generals began to spread the word around town. Now a television station contacted them to appear. Several radio stations offered them free time. Soon Ruben was preaching four times a day on the radio. The newspapers wanted a daily column from the team. Again the job fell to Ruben. A general told the team, "I can see that what you preach is the only deterrent to Communism in this country. That is why we make the city open to you."

The jail services continued every day. Then Ruben was preaching in the evening services at a church. In between, the team kept on going door-to-door. When it came time to return to the United States, Ruben felt like he had stretched his brain and abilities far beyond any limit they had known before.

He got in one of the YWAM vehicles and someone handed him all his summer's mail. His folks had mailed their letters to Nicaragua thinking he would be there. He opened them one by one. As he read the last one, he learned that while he was ministering day and night in Tegucigalpa, his little Puerto Rican grandmother had died. It was the longest, hardest trip home that Ruben was ever to experience.

Once again when Ruben got home, churches began to invite him to hold meetings. This time the crusades were in Spanish-speaking churches throughout the west. In the spring, he got a letter from the director of the YWAM Central American team, Wedge Alman. Wedge asked Ruben if he would like to accompany him on a trip back to Central America to set up Summer of Service for 1967.

"Sure!" Ruben wrote back.

Back in Honduras, they decided to split up so that they could cover more territory. So Wedge went one way and Ruben and the missionary went another. One time they packed in on horseback to a remote mountain village where the missionary left Ruben to hold meetings and do door-to-door witnessing.

The homes were wooden shacks with grass roofs and dirt floors. But since he was the visiting evangelist, Ruben was housed in the little store. The first night, Ruben put his air

"They packed in on horseback to a remote mountain village."

mattress on top of the little counter and tried to sleep. He didn't dare turn for fear he would fall off. But the noise of the big rats running around kept him off the floor.

The second night he was too tired to care. He put the air mattress down on the floor, and lay down. He could hear the rats running beside him, but his toes remained intact and he was able to sleep.

He really enjoyed his time in the little village, in spite of the rats. The meetings were packed to capacity each night with peasant folk who wanted to hear about Jesus Christ. He never forgot the sight each night after the service as the people took their lanterns off the wall of the church and began making their way up the winding paths. Ruben stood outside and watched as the lights twinkled and disappeared up the dark mountainside.

The next summer Ruben went on YWAM again. Afterward, some of the pastors invited him to return to Guatemala to hold evangelistic campaigns during the winter. They even presented him with a plane ticket for the trip down. Several churches went together and bought it for him.

For seven months he ministered in Guatemala. Sometimes it was in churches, sometimes in open-air meetings. He saw hundreds of people give their lives to Christ and many miraculous healings. Sometimes it was in tiny villages. Other times he would be in front of several thousand people in football stadiums of larger cities.

In July he met the YWAM teams in Nicaragua and worked with them all summer. Then he came back to the United States with them to see his family for the first time in almost a year.

But by January the churches in Guatemala had invited him to return again. This time they purchased a round-trip ticket on the plane. Some of the meetings were in towns where he was the year before. He found many of the converts continuing in a life of serving Christ.

In San Lucas one night, three people were carried to the altar to be prayed for. Ruben prayed for them and then moved on to the others waiting in line. Later, he looked back up the line. All three were standing up, moving about, and praising God for their healing.

In Quezaltenango he was holding meetings at an evangelistic center. There was a real move of God among the people there with many decisions for Christ and also healings.

One night a man came forward to the healing line. His little girl was in his arms. She was so thin her skin seemed stretched over her bones, except for her stomach. That was swollen to a grotesque size.

The man told Ruben his story. He had brought his child into the hospital. The doctors turned him away, saying there was nothing they could do; the child was dying. So he went in desperation to the radio station where they let him give an appeal for someone to help him. A woman phoned the station and told about Ruben's meetings. So now here he was. Ruben reached out to the child and asked the Lord to heal her.

About five o'clock the next morning, Ruben came into the church as usual to pray. He looked at the people sleeping on the benches. Some would stay here every night until the crusade was over, because they lived so far away.

A child ran up to him. Ruben didn't recognize her until he looked up and saw her father approaching. The child was smiling, and her eyes were bright. Her stomach was now a normal size. The father stood with tears streaming down his face, thanking God for the life of his little girl.

VI

Ruben stayed on in Central America and worked with the YWAM teams again during the summer of 1969. He came back to San Jose later in the fall only to find that some ministers wanted him to go to Paraguay and work for a year. In January he packed his suitcase again and set out for South America.

While he was home, Ruben often passed the used car lot where he took refuge as a child. Now he found that the cars reminded him of another incident.

He was the evangelist for a girls' team on Summer of Service in Dario, Nicaragua. One night a man came swaggering into the church. Ruben could see the handle of a gun sticking out of his pocket. The man was drunk and kept talking loudly. After the service, Ruben was praying for people around the altar when the man went outside and began shooting his gun wildly.

Y-wammer Marty Villa came by about then with mail for the team. Most of the people were leaving the church so the girls were standing off reading their letters. The man came back inside and started walking toward the girls. Ruben slipped over by them.

"Get out through the side door," he said quietly, "and to the house next door."

But the girls were so busy laughing and sharing news they didn't see what was happening. Ruben walked up to the man, searching his mind for something to say. All he knew to talk about was Jesus Christ. So he started in.

"Senor, I would like to tell you about Jesus Christ and what he means to me."

The man grunted impatiently, watching the girls. Ruben kept on talking. The girls finally came to and sensed the situation so they slipped out the side door. When the man saw that he couldn't get past Ruben, he turned and walked out.

Ruben smiled and turned to Marty to talk about news of Marty's team and others. The two sat in the church and talked. Then Ruben heard a noise. They got up and looked out the door. The man was coming back from the pool hall across the street, only this time he had ten other men with him. Ruben took a firm grip on his Bible. He nodded to Marty and the two of them moved into the doorway, Ruben nearly filling it with his great size.

"So you have come to hear more about Jesus Christ," Ruben said. The men craned their necks trying to see if the girls were inside. Ruben and Marty kept on witnessing to them. Finally the men turned and started to walk away.

"But we'll be back!" they threatened as they headed toward the pool hall.

Marty turned to him. "Look, I have to get back and see how my team is doing, but I can come back here later."

Ruben smiled. "I think everything will be okay," he said, hoping he sounded confident. He knew Marty needed to be with his team.

Ruben locked and bolted the big doors to the church. He looked at them a moment. Yes, they were strong; the men couldn't get in this way. Ruben went through the side door to the courtyard. A wall went from the front of the church to the front of the next building, blocking off the courtyard and house from the street. There was a gate in the middle of the wall, though, so that people could come and go without going through the church sanctuary.

Ruben went over and looked at the gate. He saw that ten men could easily break through. "If there was just some way to block off the gate," he thought. Then he remembered the YWAM travel-all vehicle which the team was using. He could see it parked down the street.

He went upstairs and got the keys, telling the girls not to worry; there would be no more trouble. Then he went out the gate, locked it behind him, and got into the car. He drove it up as close as possible to the gate. Then he locked all the doors and climbed in the back seat.

"If they're going to try to get in that house tonight," Ruben said, "they'll have to climb over me first!"

That night, far away in Nicaragua, Ruben Vargas was sleeping on the back seat of a car again. But this time he was there because he wasn't afraid anymore.

YWAM--In a little town in the back country of Nicaragua.

Witnessing to a member of the Rastifarian sect in Jamaica.

Outdoor service in Africa.

A national pastor in Central America welcomes a team of Spanish-speaking Y-wammers.

In many countries the teams are able to hold services in the schools, reaching hundreds of children with the message of the Gospel.

Important part of Youth With A Mission work is literature saturation work in marketplaces and busy downtown areas of the many countries.

Packing into a village in the back country of Latin America to hold a service.

Mastering the art of cooking on a kerosene stove.

A team sings for the evening service in a church.

A man in Ceylon receives Gospel literature written in his own language from a Y-wammer.

Door-to-door evangelism in the Bahamas.

A Y-wammer teaches students a Gospel song in a special school service in the Caribbean.

Witnessing on the campus of University of Mexico.

On a hillside above Montego Bay, Jamaica.

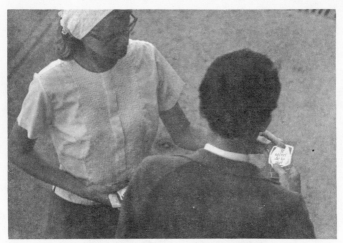

Witnessing in French-speaking Quebec.

CAMPUS REBEL

Jim rolled over carefully, eyes shut tight, trying to keep the calm of sleep inside him. Man, he wished there was a way of just falling asleep. He was so tired. Seemed like he never got to bed early. And then, on nights like this when he could, he couldn't sleep.

Slowly he opened one eye and looked at his dimly lit clock. Only eleven. A full night's sleep was possible. Why couldn't he just fall off and enjoy it? Maybe if he thought about something real blah, like trees or sky or something . . .

But just as he let his mind go, it happened. The war started again inside. It was like there was a great sea inside him that boiled up at times like this. It was a hungry, hungry sea of emptiness.

In seconds Jim was enveloped with the black loneliness which haunted him the last couple of years. Scenes from the last month came crashing back through his mind, parading relentlessly. As he remembered the moments when he was called before the college administration, the hatred for anyone in authority came over him in waves.

He remembered sitting in the office of the Director of Student Life. After a year of constant rebellious activities, the administration finally had something they could pin on him. The Director sat behind his desk, looking at Jim.

"All right, Seregow," he said. "Are you going to tell us about it?"

The black hatred boiled up again and Jim felt it so strong that he could be icy cool. He stared the man in the face.

"Well," said the man, his voice rising, "are you going to tell us about it?"

Now there was nothing but bitter hate which brought super ice inside. Jim's eyes never wavered. Fifteen minutes went by.

"Look, Seregow," the Director said finally. "Either you

tell us what happened or you can get up and walk out."

Jim walked out.

Now as he lay in bed, remorse swept over him. He really despised the hate he saw in his life. A voice seemed to come inside him. "Why are you doing these things?"

Immediately his mind went back to the Sunday services at his home church in Detroit, Michigan.

"No," cried Jim silently. "I don't want anything to do with God!" Yet even as he said it, in his mind he could see family devotions back home. Then his mind clicked over to the moment last month when he had to phone his dad. Standing there beside the phone booth he hesitated.

"Oh, come on, Seregow," he said to himself. "You've got the guts to do it. Get it over with." Quickly he put in the dime and dialed the operator. It seemed like only seconds before his father's familiar voice came on the line.

"Hi, Dad," Jim started. "You're going to be getting some letters from the college pretty soon."

"Oh," came his dad's voice, now wary.

Jim plunged ahead. "One is going to tell you I have too many chapel cuts. The next letter will tell you that I'm on academic probation. And the third letter is that I'm on character probation," he finished in a rush.

There was a long silence. Jim knew his father well enough to know what his face looked like right now. He wanted to tell him that he was sorry for the humiliation he was bringing him, but the words just wouldn't come out.

His father spoke now, his voice low and quiet. "Son, I think it's time for you to come home."

"Oh, no, Dad," Jim blurted out. "I can't. Don't you see? I've really got to stay now. I've got to make all this right again. Look, this won't happen anymore, I promise. I'm going to change, you'll see."

The phone went quiet again for a while. "All right," his Dad said finally, his voice sounding tired.

Jim hung up. He'd do it. He really would make something better of his life. He knew he could.

His resolve lasted about two weeks, and then it was back to the old life. He even tried to be nice to the professors and administration, but he just couldn't do it. One day after the

"As long as he kept busy in some kind of trouble his mind didn't bother him."

new semester, Jim put his head down and tried to get some sleep in history class. He hadn't been in Dr. Ulibarri's classes before, but it didn't matter.

"Jim Seregow!" Dr. Ulibarri called out.

Jim sat straight up in surprise.

"In this class you take notes and stay awake or you're out," the professor said.

Jim looked up defiantly. "What matter is it of yours as long as I'm here?" he yelled back.

Now, in the darkness of his room, the whole thing seemed like a bad dream. He wished the emptiness would go away. Man, what would the other guys think if they knew he had times like these? He tried to concentrate on that thought because the void was rising up again and he could hardly stand it. Nothing he could do would make it go away. Silently, in the darkness, Jim shook with sobs and didn't know why.

Yet the next night, when a gang of students started talking about another campus disturbance, Jim eagerly joined in on the plans. As long as he kept busy in some kind of trouble, his mind didn't bother him.

At lunch one day, a buddy came up. "Hey, Seregow," he grinned. "Have you seen what's going on in the English department?"

"No, what," said Jim, barely looking up.

"Man, they're having a revival. Some teacher was opening class this morning by having a student pray and everybody started praying."

Jim felt a chill run through him. One of the reasons he came to this college was that he knew there would always be people around who could pray, in case he needed it quick some day.

"Do you want to check out the action with me?" asked his friend.

"Not me!" Jim replied. "I've had all the religion I can take."

As he watched his friend walk away, Jim almost changed his mind. It would be interesting. Kathy, his former girl friend, would probably be right in the thick of it. She always was when it came to anything about God. He remembered back in high school when everything was smooth between them. It was always fun to be with her then, Kathy with her dancing blue eyes and great sense of humor. But everything changed when she came here to college. When he followed the second semester, he found that their relationship had changed. She was in just about everything at the college, all kinds of committees and social functions. Every time he wanted to talk to her, someone was always interrupting.

Finally, when he did get her off all to himself and start talking about the two of them or his interest in cars, she'd change the subject to something about God. One day as they walked through the fields on a botany field trip, Jim had all he could stand. Kathy was chattering about some new school function when Jim exploded.

"All you ever think about is what your friends want for your life!" he yelled. And when the tirade of angry words finally emptied out, he realized he had taken hard, crushing words to shatter their relationship completely. It was then, when Kathy turned and walked away through the green grass, that Jim felt that empty sea boil up so high inside him that it seemed to completely engulf him.

Now, as Jim walked toward his dorm, he tried to shake off the memory. He must find something to do and get rid of this depression. That episode with Kathy happened over a year ago. He could live without her or anyone else's help. Let them have their revival.

But by the time supper was over, Jim's curiosity couldn't take much more. Everyone was talking about it, for they'd all been over to the English wing sometime during the day. Now there were supposed to be four hundred kids over there praying.

Slowly Jim headed out the cafeteria toward the English department. He'd just walk by on his way to the dorm. He came to the entrance and began walking through. There were kids in every classroom. Everyone was praying and worshiping the Lord. Some of the professors were in there with them.

At one room, Jim looked in the door, straight into the faces of kids praying with faces upturned, tears streaming down their cheeks. That voice came inside him again. "Maybe this is your hour to face God."

"Oh, no you don't," said Jim and turned and ran outside, into the darkness. When he finally stopped running, he walked and walked, unable to erase the sight of the students' faces from his mind. The void was rising up again and it was getting more and more demanding. For a moment he wished that he could, just for one second, feel the peace inside that those kids seemed to have.

He glanced at his watch. Nine o'clock. He'd been walking for three hours. He'd better get back to his dorm. "I'll just go by the English department and see if it's going on still," he thought. "But this time, Seregow, stay outside!"

When he got there, he stopped and looked in a window. Just then someone came up behind him. Before he could turn around, a hand touched him gently on the shoulder. He spun around and came face to face with Dr. Ulibarri.

"Jim," he said quietly, "do you want to go in and pray?"

"No. No, man," said Jim shaking his head. "I don't want to go in there."

"How about one of the other rooms?" the professor persisted gently.

Jim hesitated. Then the huge emptiness rose up again. It would not be put off.

"Okay," he said. "But somewhere by ourselves."

They found an empty room and Jim fell to his knees. "Oh, God," he wept. "Oh, Father God, forgive me." And there poured out of his heart all that had been held back: all the rebellion, all the hate, all the defiance as he pled with God to once again make him His child.

Then all grew quiet inside. Slowly a wonderful peace came over him. It went right to the empty place and began to fill up. Joy welled up inside as he began to feel the Holy Spirit coming back into his life. He hadn't appreciated that joy before when he worshiped God as a child. But now he knew the price of it, and it became a full cup from which he drank with thanksgiving.

Just before he got up from his knees, Jim made God a promise. "I don't know what it will take to serve You, God," he prayed, "for I don't know what You want from my life. But I never want to go back to what I was. I commit my life to You."

It was late at night when he finally made his way back to his room. As he neared the dorm he stopped and looked at it with new sight. "It's still the same place," he thought. "The same guys are in there, some of them doing all the things that I did just hours ago. I'm going to have to live this new life in front of them. They'll watch every move I make."

Suddenly he felt helpless. He knew he didn't have the strength in himself to live this new life because he had tried before and failed. "Okay, God," he prayed silently. "I'll spend time reading Your Word every day, and I'll get on my knees each day and pray until I feel Your presence in my life.

II

Throughout the next year, Jim continued his walk with God. During the spring semester a young man spoke in chapel one day. His name was Loren Cunningham. He told of an opportunity for young people to go to islands in the Caribbean that summer to do personal witnessing. He represented a group called Youth With A Mission. He stressed that before anyone could join, they had to know that God had called them. Also, the participants had to pay their own way.

Jim prayed and signed up.

When the young people got to the Virgin Islands, they were divided up into teams. Each member was given a specific job for the summer such as literature, food, or follow-up. Loren came up to Jim.

"I want you to be a team captain," he said.

Jim looked at him. He knew the duties of a captain. It meant he had to be responsible for the rest of the team in every way. He had to find them lodging in a strange town if necessary. He was to see that they never ran out of supplies. The full responsibility of his team's performance during the summer would be on his shoulders.

"All right," he said; then he went off to pray. "Oh, God," he prayed. "I need Your guidance and strength as never before. I trust You to show me how to be a leader and what to do this summer." Then he went out to meet his team.

They went to the island of Tortolla first. There they went door-to-door at little wooden shanties, talking to people about Jesus Christ. The rest of the summer was spent on smaller islands like Jost Van Dyke, doing the same thing.

When the teams headed out, they were given a few dollars to use as change in the literature fund. They were also given a supply of canned and dried food. That was it. They were to trust God for their other needs such as transportation, fresh fruit, and housing.

Jim saw many people give their lives to Christ that summer. He also saw God undertake for the team's daily needs, many times in miraculous ways. By the end of the summer he was convinced that God really did work through people and would answer the prayer of a sincere heart.

Jim returned to college in the fall. His confidence as a leader must have shown, for they asked him to be resident assistant of the athletic dorm. It was the prestige dorm, filled with the college athletes. It would be a tough place, for many of the fellows were big and outspoken.

Jim held his first meeting with the fellows. "I promise you that I'll deal with each of you honestly and fairly," he said as he handed them a list of the rules. "And it means that I will hold you to the rules of the school."

The first semester was hard. The boys would do things just to agitate Jim. He was determined to keep the spirit of Christ in dealing with them. But it was hard.

One night he found himself pounding on the bed silently and praying, "God, if I go out there now I'm gonna hit them!"

The noise continued. He knew he couldn't deal with them until his own heart was settled. Quickly he went out of the dormitory and to the prayer chapel.

"Oh, Father, help me now," he prayed. He realized he was being tested to the breaking point.

The Spirit of the Lord seemed to come over him. Like a medicine it began to ebb away the frustration. Jim waited before the Lord, drawing strength from His presence. He began to think of the fellows again. For the first time, he really loved them. As each one's face came before him, he began to look at their problems. He knew why they acted the way they did. He had just ignored it before. Now he wanted to go back and begin helping each one.

At the end of the year, a young man took him for a ride one day.

"Seregow," he said. "I just wanted to tell you that I've watched you all this year. You've made more of an impact on my life than all the training, chapel services, or anything else. If you can make it, anybody can!"

After church one night, Jim knelt in prayer. He knew that it was time to face up to something he had avoided for months. He meant it when he gave his life to the Lord two years ago, but he knew that there was one word he needed to say in commitment. He was scared. He had never put himself out on a limb like this with God before.

"Dear God," he began. "If You want me in the ministry, I'm willing to go."

Then he waited. Nothing happened. No blinding flash or vision, just an amazing peace about the whole thing. Then came a sense of being highly privileged because God wanted to use him.

"It's not hard," he thought as he got off his knees. "It's really terrific!" He was almost laughing now. He had been so scared to give in to God, and it didn't hurt, not one bit.

Jim kept his major in education but he changed his minor to religion and philosophy as he began to prepare himself for the ministry.

Jim worked out in California the next summer, filling gallon cans of fruit cocktail in a cannery. He also went to night school to pick up the course he failed back east. And he applied for a license to minister.

In midsummer he went to Santa Cruz to appear before the Presbytery for his ministerial interview. Several other young men were in the waiting room with him. Some of them made up a group called "Disciples Three." They worked during the day and witnessed on the Berkeley campus of the University of California at night. They sang folk songs they had composed and gave their testimonies. The three of them were talking.

"Wouldn't it be something if we had to give our lives for Christ?" one said. "Wouldn't that be fantastic?"

Jim turned and looked at the group. "Man, these guys are weird," he thought.

But he saw that they really felt they would enjoy dying for Christ. They considered it a privilege.

Jim sat and thought about it a moment. He had always wanted to get to a place in God where he wouldn't care about public opinion or pressures. He often longed for the strength to be able to stand for Christ wherever he was.

"These guys have that," he thought. "And I want it."

He continued to question the young men about their work until they invited him to come up to Berkeley and see what it was like. He accepted eagerly and went up the first chance he got. He stood near the great iron gates of the campus, watching the thousands of young students pass by. He looked at their faces, amazed at their open interest in each speaker. The great white buildings of the university loomed up behind the Disciples Three as they sang and talked to the young people. Jim saw the potential for reaching the young people of America and he knew he wanted to do this kind of work more than anything in the world.

III

Jim returned to his own college in the fall and finished his last semester. Then he went to Michigan where he worked as a field representative for Youth With A Mission. He conducted weekend crusades in towns around Michigan, Ohio, and Ontario, Canada. When not in crusades he did substitute teaching. But the main reason he came back to Michigan was that Kathy was teaching in Flint. They had dated off and on during their last years in college and now Jim knew he wanted to marry her.

"I believe we should get married," he told her one night.

"Well, the Lord will have to confirm it to me," she replied. They had been through too much to take the step lightly. So Jim went home and waited. The answer was two months in coming. But when it came, it was "Yes."

They decided to go on Youth With A Mission's Summer Of Service again that year. As Jim worked in Jamaica, once again he was impressed with the potential of what young people could accomplish for God.

He returned home to marry Kathy, knowing there was a place for them to work on YWAM full time if it was God's will. But over and over again the scene of the students on campus came to him.

"What if we took the techniques of Youth With A Mission and applied them to a university campus?" he thought one night. "We could go door-to-door in the dorms, talking to the kids personally about Jesus Christ." The very thought kept him awake with excited plans. But God hadn't shown him specifically where He wanted them to work.

So Jim and Kathy went to work teaching full time, waiting for God's next move. One night Jim went into the living room of their little flat to pray. He was waiting before the Lord when a picture of the University of Michigan campus came into his mind. He could see the students walking through the Diag at the center of the campus. Then he saw young people in teams going through the campus and standing before crowds to profess Jesus Christ.

Jim got up from his knees. Now it was more than just a feeling. God had shown him the place to begin his ministry. He just needed to know when.

That summer Jim and Kathy took four college students and formed a group they called the "New Life Team." They helped minister in small churches and did door-to-door evangelism in different towns of Michigan.

At the end of the summer, Jim and Kathy returned to their home and made plans for a quick trip to California to see his parents. One day the phone rang. The caller was a lady whom they knew casually, but she had never called before.

"Jim," she said, "I've been praying and I have received a message from God that I am to call you and tell you to take up the gauntlet. I don't know what you're praying about but God wants you to take up the challenge."

Jim hung up the phone, his heart pounding with excitement. If this indeed was the time, then he must step out. But how was he to begin? He felt that they were supposed to start at the University of Michigan in Ann Arbor, but he sure would like some confirmation.

"Let's stop by Ann Arbor on our way to California," he

said to Kathy. "If we can find an apartment there, then we'll take it as from the Lord."

"Find an apartment in Ann Arbor this time of year?" said friends. "The returning students snatched them up long ago. Besides, the prices of rent are outrageous in college towns."

When Jim and Kathy got to Ann Arbor, they found that they had only two hours to spare before taking off for California.

"Lord," prayed Jim. "This is it. We've got to get an apartment. It's got to be furnished and it's got to be something we can afford." Then Jim and Kathy looked at each other. If God had really called them, they would know within two hours.

It took even less time to find it. The apartment was fully furnished, with a low rent that included utilities. They moved into the apartment a few weeks later. As soon as he could, Jim set out for the campus.

"Well, I'm here," he thought as he walked along. "But where do I begin?" He had given a name to the outreach, Campus Action. And he had some churches behind him, promising their support. He just needed to start the ball rolling.

His walk brought him to the center of campus known as the Diag. He watched the students milling around the literature tables which various radical and militant groups maintained. He saw how people would hand out leaflets and newspapers to the students who walked through. Everywhere he looked, he saw the young students pausing to read the literature.

"What if I wrote up something appropriate to the college scene but brought in the message of Christ and His love?" he thought. He knew they would spot a Gospel tract a mile away and treat it with disdain. But what if it was something in their own media, written especially to them?

He hurried home and began to write. The word treason, had been bothering him for days as he watched the students demonstrate. Now he began to write about it.

"Peace, peace, peace!" "Hell no, we won't go." The cry for peace rings out amid the turmoil and aggression of one nation against another. But can there be a lasting peace?

Peace on earth will never come until there is peace in man's heart, Jim continued. *Love and freedom will not come until one subjects himself to the highest of all governments in existence, the moral government of God.* Jim went on to explain how a young person can use his intellect and sovereignty to choose between right and wrong to find God.

When he finished, he took the copy down to the local church that was helping sponsor him. He got out a pile of paper and began to mimeograph his leaflet. He used a regular size sheet of paper and folded it in half with the word "Treason" printed on the outside in bold letters. Then he printed the message inside. He worked diligently until he ran off five hundred of them.

"That's plenty for a while," he decided, and put the machine away.

He went back to the Diag, five hundred copies of his message in his arms. "What if no one takes it?" he thought. He could see himself standing there all day, feeling stupid with an armful of leaflets, while forty thousand students walked by.

He walked near the center and stood waiting. Some students walked up, looking at the literature.

"Hey, look at this," one of them called. "Treason! Yeah, we buy that. Gimme some more of those."

Within minutes, Jim was standing there empty-handed.

That night after he got home, the phone rang. It was a young man who said his name was Carl.

"Look," Carl said. "My wife and I have read your Treason leaflet. You say we shouldn't march or demonstrate to bring about peace. So what should we do?"

"The desire for peace is a real one," Jim answered. "But true peace can come only when there's a spiritual revolution within the heart of man so that his motivation changes from one of selfishness to one of love."

"I see," Carl answered.

"Look, Carl," Jim went on. "We can put down war in Vietnam, racism in Detroit, and crime in Ann Arbor. But they always spring up somewhere else because they're just symptons of the real problem, selfishness. Individual selfishness breeds national selfishness. And that in turn breeds international selfishness."

"That's very interesting," Carl replied. "I'd like to talk to you more about this."

Jim invited Carl and his wife to come to a Bible study meeting which he was starting in conjunction with the witnessing work. They came and listened to him. Afterward Carl came up to Jim.

"Say, this is really great," he said. "I want to join your group."

"You can only join one way, Carl," said Jim. "That's by being born into the group." Then he got his Bible and showed Carl the third chapter of John with the story of Nicodemus. That night, Carl and his wife asked Christ to set up His Kingdom in their hearts.

The second day of his experiment with the leaflets, Jim prepared one thousand copies. Once again he watched in amazement as they disappeared within minutes. The next day he tried it with two thousand. Then three thousand, four thousand, and finally five thousand copies at a time.

"You know," he said to Kathy afterward, "on any given day, two or three Christian young people could completely saturate a campus with their message and get the students talking about it."

He began to write other leaflets tying in current problems with the message of Jesus Christ. He did them all in the same format, one word outside and the message inside. Soon "Revolutionist," "Absolute," and other leaflets began appearing all over the campus of the university. The job of mimeographing got so big that Jim had to begin having them printed professionally.

One day a Jewish student picked up a leaflet entitled "Hypocrite" from the table in the Diag. He put it under the door of Leo, a Catholic friend of his, for a joke. But it was no joke to Leo. He was searching for truth in his life. Leo called Jim up and asked him to come over. Jim did, and they talked for many hours. Then Leo came out to the meetings Jim was conducting. Jim continued to visit him and talk about the reality of a Christ-filled life.

One day Leo said to him, "I'm going to bring my Bible when I return from vacation."

Several nights later, Jim was holding a meeting at the north campus. There were about fifteen fellows in the room when Leo walked in. Jim was talking about the prophecies concerning Israel in the Bible and showing how they were coming to pass.

"If a person was going to get his heart right with God, now would be the time to do it," said Jim. "No one knows how much time he has left in this life."

"Yes, do it now," came a voice. "Accept Christ now!"

Jim looked up. There sat Leo doing the talking. "What does he mean?" thought Jim, and he tried to quiet him down. But Leo kept interrupting.

"You should do it. You as an individual should do it today."

Jim brought the meeting to a quick close and went over to Leo. "What happened to you?" he asked.

"Well, at home over the Easter holiday I began to think about all you told me," Leo said. "I decided you were either crazy or that you honestly had peace in your heart."

Jim smiled.

"Well, I knew you weren't crazy, and I really believe that you have a peace. So I got down beside my bed and began to read my Bible. Then I asked Christ to come into my heart. Now I want to tell everybody about it!"

Each week brought more phone calls from both students and professors who wanted to find out more about what Jim and Kathy believed. Soon Jim developed a follow-up program to help the new believers grow in the Lord. They got the religious preference cards of the student body and began recruiting born-again Christian students to work with them. They went door-to-door in dormitories, continued literature tables in the Diag, did follow-up work, and constantly stayed on the alert for new opportunities to bring the message of Christ to the campus.

Today the outreach has spread to the campuses of Michigan, State, Central Michigan University, Ferris State and many others. A summer program called "Summer Of Action" has been started. Christian students from different states and campuses come to work full time for eight weeks to spread the good news of Christ to their fellow collegians.

Jim has been on a college campus for many years now. Maybe he'll be there the rest of his life. He doesn't know and doesn't care. He has joined a special revolution and found the answers to his life in it. Now he wants every other young person in the world to hear about it too.

THE CATALYST

It never occurred to Loren Cunningham that hearing the voice of God might be a unique experience. When he was thirteen he thought that nearly every Christian experienced it. Mainly it was because that was the way he had grown up. Whenever his folks were faced with a decision, they prayed for God's leading on the matter—like when God led them to their first pastorate.

His folks were praying one day and the Lord showed them a map and a town on it that they didn't know existed. They set off for the place and came into the back of the little church there the following Sunday. When the pastor found out his dad was a minister, he asked him to preach. After the service they found out that the pastor had resigned with the assurance that God would send someone else to take his place. And sure enough, the church voted the Cunninghams in as pastors.

Loren's folks were like that because of their parents. Grandpa Cunningham was known throughout the Midwestern states as the "Walking Bible." He could quote whole chapters at a time. Loren's Grandpa Nicholson was a real fireball of an Irish preacher. He always liked to hear Grandpa Nicholson preach because he never knew what he would say or do next. Grandpa was a hot-tempered drunkard until he gave his life to God one morning at the breakfast table. Right after that, God called him to preach so he bundled up the five kids and Grandma into a covered wagon and set out to minister wherever God led him.

It was a way of life for the Nicholson kids to start the day with prayer. Maybe it was because Grandpa was so sincere about it. Even when the kids prayed for someone in the service, they would see miracles and healings. When some of the children would get into a fight, Granddad would send them out into the fields to "pray through" before they could come back. When they wanted to do something, Granddad would say, "You go out and pray about it and see what God tells you to do."

When they came back and told him what God had said about the matter, Granddad would say, "All right."

And that was the way Loren's mom treated him and his sisters as they grew up. So when he felt the Lord speaking to him when he was praying one night when he was thirteen, he just said, "Yes." The Lord brought to his mind the words, *"Go ye into all the world and preach the gospel to every creature."* It stood out in Loren's mind in great big letters. He knew for sure he wasn't making it up when he opened his eyes and the words were still there. So Loren said, "Yes," and got up off his knees assuming that someday God would send him into the world to do just that.

In the meantime he went on to high school, joined his buddies in going out for sports, and invited them to come hear his dad preach. Then one day Loren saw a confirmation to his call. He was down in Mexico with some other college-age kids during Easter vacation. Their trip had been paid for by Pop Jenkins, a Christian man in Fresno, California. The guys were camping out and sleeping on the ground at night. Then all day they were busy giving out thousands of pieces of literature and witnessing the best they could in their high school Spanish.

On the last day, the fellows finished their work and started driving back to California. As Loren looked back at the last pueblo, he knew that the memory of brown hands reaching out for literature and of people who would actually kneel on the street to accept Christ would remain forever in his mind. "If we could accomplish all of that in one week," he thought, "what could a group of kids do in one month or a year?"

Even as he thought it, the words of Mark 16:15 came to him again and he knew for certain that God had spoken to him that night five years before.

That summer Loren heard the voice of the Lord again. He was working thirty-six hours a week at Ralph's, a Southern California chain grocery store. He was also going to summer school at college, piling up as many units as he could. Besides this, he was engaged to be married. He had bought furniture

"The memory of . . . people who would actually kneel on the street to accept Christ would remain forever in his mind."

and appliances and even been able to put a down payment on a house. But one night, very clearly and very definitely the Lord said, "No."

Then God began to show Loren that he was going against His plan and once again pointed out the call Loren had received. So Loren broke his engagement, sold every possession, and went back east to Bible college to prepare his life for the ministry.

In school Loren took as many classes as he could, picking them by the teacher who taught them. He added to his education by the practical experience of singing in a traveling quartet. In the summer, his quartet would strike out on their own. They would set up their itinerary, do their own preaching, and live off their offerings. (It was this last area which required the most faith!)

That same year the quartet traveled to the Bahama Islands for some services. They were sitting in a home talking one day when the conversation turned to the news that there was another group of kids on an out island who had come to do missionary work.

Loren sat up and began to listen with interest. A missionary spoke. "Well, you know these young kids," he said. "They want to do something for the Lord so they come out here. But all they're doing is floundering."

Loren turned to the man and almost spoke but then stopped. He didn't want to sound impertinent. "If someone would just give these kids some guidance," he thought, "they could do an effective job."

He didn't remember the incident again until later that year, back in college. Alfred Cawston, a returned missionary from India, was standing before a class talking about world conditions.

"If we are ever going to see the world evangelized," he said earnestly, "then *everybody* has got to get involved. That means laymen and young people, too."

Loren sat there, a shiver of excitement going through him. He remembered the moment coming home from Mexico and his excitement at the potential of young people. Then his mind jumped to the moment in the Bahamas last summer. "There must be a way of overcoming the problem and using this great potential working force," he thought. But no plans came to his mind.

II

The thought that young people could have more of a place in the Kingdom of God recurred over and over again to Loren during the next three years, but it would soon fade away in the rush of his full life. He had a call of God to fulfill and he wanted to be prepared.

After Loren graduated from Bible college, his Aunt Sandra made it financially possible for him to comtinue his education at the University of Southern California. By the fall of 1959 he had three BA degrees to his name in the fields of Bible, Christian Education and Philosophy, and he was hard at work on his Master's degree. He had everything done except his thesis. At the same time he was working as an assistant pastor in a large church in Inglewood, California. He was also busy participating in the district programs of his denomination.

One day before Christmas, he went across Los Angeles to take care of some business in Pasadena. He had just come out of a bank when he met an old friend of his, Roy Sapp.

"How are you doing?" smiled Roy.

"Fine, and how are things with you?" answered Loren. The two fell into a discussion of their work. Roy was the Southern California president of the young people's organization for their church.

"You know, Loren," said Roy thoughtfully, "there's a lot of power here in young people if we could just channel it the right way."

Loren's eyes lit up. "I'd like to share with you what I've been thinking along these lines," he said, and began to tell him some of his experiences during the previous years.

"The young people I work with now," he went on, "really seem to be frustrated. They are almost desperate to serve the Lord in some capacity."

"I know," nodded Roy. "I see it in the church youth rallies all the time."

Loren's mind went back to his times of counseling young

people after a consecration service. "What can I do?" they would ask. He always tried to start out with the right approach, that church work requires them to have a college degree usually, so that they should prepare in this way. Also that before a person could become a missionary, he must have two or three years of ministry in the United States. But the kids would always interrupt him impatiently.

"Today our kids want something they can do right now," observed Loren. "They seem to need a cause and if the church doesn't give it to them, I'm convinced they will look until they find it somewhere else."

The two men fell silent for a moment, listening to the wind rattle the street decorations overhead. Loren was remembering the time in Mexico and how it had challenged his life. "You know, it would be great if we could take a large number of kids into Mexico to evangelize," he mused out loud.

Roy looked at him quickly. "If you want to take it on as a project, you go ahead and I'll back you up."

"Okay," said Loren. "I'll do it."

By the following spring Loren had found that the costs of taking a boat down the coast would be more than chartering a plane to fly 100 people to Hawaii. So he made plans to charter a plane during Easter vacation. 106 young people went with the group to Honolulu.

On the long flight home, Loren and Roy sat together, sharing their reactions to the work of the kids. "I think our main problem was that even though we had services lined up for each night, most of the group seemed to be tourist-oriented," said Loren.

"I know what you mean," answered Roy. "There was only a small core of this bunch who had come with the motivation to put all of their efforts into evangelism."

"But you take those forty," said Loren. "If we had come with just those, we could have accomplished just as much. You know, if we had a screening process with a set of values, so that people were aware of the idea of discipleship being required..." Then he stopped, embarrassed. He suddenly realized that he was talking like a leader of a group or program and he most certainly wasn't. He was a busy young man, with many things to accomplish yet.

Within months, a trip around the world worked out for him. He was really excited about it, for he was going as a missionary-evangelist. As he traveled, he couldn't get over the great work missionaries were accomplishing. Everywhere he went, he spoke before people crowded into buildings with the overflow crowd peering through windows from the outside.

Each country brought added interest to him. The sound of a strange tongue and the foreign culture was exhilarating. Day on day piled up behind him: the plane taking off for a new land; the plane landing; people smiling and greeting him; the eager faces of a church congregation clapping as they welcomed this American preacher. At night it was the faces of those who came to the front to publicly accept Jesus Christ.

One night in New Delhi, he jumped into the car with his host, Bob Marion, to drive down to the marketplace. As they rode along, suddenly Bob stopped the car. "Look over there, Loren. There's a ceremony going on at the burning grounds. Would you like to go in and see it?"

"Yes!" said Loren, eager for this opportunity. They climbed out of the car and entered the dark grounds. The stench of burning flesh hung in the air. A group of people, wild-eyed with grief and terror, were running around trying to drive the evil spirits from the body of a teen-age boy who had died in a knifing.

Loren moved closer until he was standing inside the circle of running people. The priests were running with them, their long robes making them seem even stranger in the flickering torch light. Loren felt like he was standing in the circle of nirvana—the circle of emptiness. Just then in his mind, he saw the crowded street which he had just left. Then past that to the streets of Hong Kong and Tokyo, always crowded with a mass of humanity on the move. Against that scene he put the churches filled to capacity with eager listeners and saw very clearly that there was still much more work to be done in the world.

Well, he was only one. But he would keep traveling, keep preaching, keep witnessing to people personally until his life gave out. Maybe it wasn't much, but God had said to go, so he would. "And when I get back home," he thought, "I'll tell of this need to every young person I meet."

The burden for a greater Gospel witness in the world grew now with each succeeding country until it was like a giant worm eating away inside him. So when he got home, he would talk and preach for an hour or more, in his excitement to share his experiences so that other young people would get excited about missions, too.

His first series of services was in Bakersfield, California. One night after the service, the kids invited him to go out to eat with them. He accepted eagerly. Here was a chance at last to talk personally with them. They drove over to the hamburger stand in Dallas Moore's car. Loren couldn't help noticing how proud he was of it. He had really fixed it up and souped up the motor, pointing out to Loren the many improvements he had made in it.

They finished ordering the food and Loren thought, "Here's my chance now to work on these guys," and he launched into one of his adventures around the world. They smiled politely but the conversation soon shifted back to talk of cars.

Loren decided to try again. "Maybe they just need to hear some more," he thought. But once again the subject shifted back to their interests. And so it went during the evening. By the time Loren got back to the car he could hardly keep from showing his frustration.

"What are these guys thinking?" he fumed silently. "Don't they know a whole world is in desperate need and all they can talk about is cars and new clothes?"

The answer was several months in coming. In the meantime he was asked to speak at a youth convention for the Southern California district. Before the end of the convention, he came up with an idea. "Why not have kids fill our cards with their commitment at the end of the dedication service?" he mused. "Then we could mail them back one year later and they could measure their lives."

The suggestion was followed, and after the final service, Loren sat with some of the other youth leaders, reading over the cards. Loren looked down at the card in his hand. "I am willing and would even be glad for the chance to die for Christ," a young person had written. Loren looked at the next card. It said almost the same thing. Teen-ager after teen-ager had put in writing an intense desire to really do something for the Kingdom of God, something that would last.

That night Loren rode back home with friend, Bob Theetge. All during the trip his mind kept going back to the commitments on those cards. He turned to Bob. "Man, we've got to do something. There must be some way we could get these young people moving into service for God," he said, his mind searching for a key. "Bob, we've got to give these kids some place to work; it's not enough just to challenge them and leave it at that."

"Well, let's do it, Loren," said Bob.

Loren looked over at his friend. "Really? You mean organize something ourselves?"

"Yes," said Bob. "I'll help you. What have we got to do?"

Loren sank back in his seat. "Bob, you don't realize what you're getting into. You're a businessman with many demands on your time already. Surely you don't really mean . . ."

Bob's face was set. "Let's go," he said quietly.

By January of 1961 five men were meeting together and trying to organize a youth program which they were now calling Youth With A Mission. Loren and Roy Sapp went back east to their denominational headquarters and presented the program there to get approval. First they would have outreaches for evangelism by young people in the United States, Loren explained. Then they would have summer programs where kids would go to foreign countries and work.

But even while he talked, he could see that there was a definite hesitation. He knew the questions that were going over in their minds. "How will zealous young people with little head knowledge react to a strange culture?" "What about the mistakes they will make?" "They have so little training." Loren knew he didn't have any answers; yet something inside him was demanding that it be done and he couldn't turn back.

Finally one of the brethren made the remark that he

would be even happier if Loren could provide them with someone who could give vocational help on the mission field.

"You would?" asked Loren. "Is that what you really need?"

"Yes!" came the answer. "We need schoolteachers, nurses, road builders—people who can give the missionaries more time for evangelism."

"All right," said Loren. "I believe we can get them."

All the way back home Loren made plans. They would call the program "Vocational Volunteers." Sure it wasn't waves of young people going out to do personal evangelism, but it was a beginning. As soon as he got home he would start lining up services to challenge young people.

One of his first recruitment services happened to be back in Bakersfield. Loren challenged the kids that night, telling of teaching opportunities in other lands, and of a road that missionaries needed built for a leper colony in Africa. After the service some of the young people came forward to pray. Later several came over to talk to Loren. One of the first was Dallas Moore and his friend, Larry Hendricks.

"God has spoken to us about going to Africa and building that road," he said. "Larry and I drive heavy road equipment for a living. It's just the job for us."

Loren looked at the young man he had written off in disgust a few months before. "But—but—" he stammered. "How could you get money for such a trip?" he finally asked, unable to believe what was happening.

"Oh, that's easy," smiled Dallas. "I can sell my car."

III

Loren was busy in services all spring. When the thought would occasionally slip into his mind that this was an awfully slow beginning for such a big vision, he would promptly dismiss it. When summer came, he had another chance to travel. This time he set off for Russia, then flew on down to Africa. One of his stops there was in Kedougu, Senegal, where he met missionary Talmadge Butler, his wife, and son. All day Loren and Talmadge would travel by jeep to outlying villages, bringing them the Gospel. In the evening they would return to Kedougu, which was the market town for the area, and Loren would preach in a service at the church.

One night after church, Loren and Talmadge sat at the little kitchen table, waiting as Marge served up their nightly treat of yogurt made with powdered milk. Loren looked past the light of the little lantern on the table, thinking back over the incidents of the day.

"That was really something," he said aloud, "when the people applauded this morning. When you told me that the next village had never heard the Gospel before, I was really excited at first. It was the kind of experience I always dreamed about when I was a kid. But as we drove along, then I began to realize the responsibility of it."

"I know what you mean," smiled Talmadge. "Kinda scary, isn't it?"

Loren grinned. Then Talmadge turned to his wife. "You should have been there, Marge. Loren had just finished telling these people that there was only one true God and that He loved them so much he had sent His only Son to die for their sins when all of a sudden the people began to clap and cheer."

"Loren, how wonderful!" cried Marge. "What did you do?"

"For a moment there, I was so moved I could hardly go on speaking," Loren admitted. "I never want to forget the experience. I just wish . . ."

"Wish what?" Talmadge asked in interest.

"Oh, I was just thinking about an aunt of mine—something she said to me before I left on this trip."

"Well?"

"It was my Aunt Sandra. She's the one who put me through college."

"Terrific!" smiled Talmadge. "How did it happen?"

"It was the fall of my senior year in Bible college," Loren said. "I had just met her that summer when I was in Lake Placid, New York, traveling with the quartet. She had been out of touch with the family while we were growing up.

"Anyway, back at school in September, I was down at the creek praying one day, asking God for the assurance that I was to stay in school. You know, we hadn't made any money on our quartet travels," he laughed, "so I had come back broke. Well, I got up off my knees after praying this and was walking across the campus. Someone came out of a building and called to me, telling me that I had a long-distance phone call. It was Aunt Sandra calling to find out if she could pay my school bill that year!"

"Isn't the Lord wonderful to us?" smiled Marge as she set the yogurt before them.

Loren stirred his and took a bite, slowly savoring it. "When I was starting off on this trip, I stopped by to see her a few days. It was then that she suggested I come to the east to live with them and work in their business."

"That sounds interesting," said Talmadge.

"I guess it was, now that I think about it," sighed Loren. "But it really didn't seem like it at the time. I remember I just told her as gently as I could that I had a calling and felt that I must do what God directed me to do."

"What did she say to that?"

"Well, that's when she didn't understand. I remember how puzzled her face became, wondering why I couldn't fulfill a calling by living in the United States. That's why I was wishing she could have been there today. I think that she would have understood what I was trying to explain to her . . . maybe," finished Loren lamely.

Talmadge caught it and looked up. "Maybe?" he grinned.

"Oh, nothing, really," Loren answered, but even as he said it, his mind returned to the conversation with his aunt.

"Why can't you minister in the United States?" she had asked him.

"Well, Aunt Sandra," he said as he looked down at her "it has to do with my call when I was thirteen." Then he had gone on and told her about the verse.

Her eyebrows shot up. "Oh, Loren, you can't take that literally. How can God mean for you to reach every person on earth? You know it's impossible."

Loren had never thought of it that way before. He just stood there without an answer. Was he trying to do something that was impossible? Before he could think of anything to say, the butler saved the moment by announcing dinner.

But even now as he sat here in Africa, he knew he still didn't have an answer. "Tell me, Talmadge," he said. "Does God ask you to do something that is impossible?"

Talmadge's eyes lit up. "Sometimes I get that feeling when I look around us here in Senegal," he laughed. Then he grew serious. "Loren, you've already seen what you can do in just the few days you've been here. Yet out beyond that village where we were today, are hundreds and hundreds more just like it."

Loren sighed. "It seems almost unbellievable in this modern time."

"But it's true," said Talmadge. "We've got 55,000 people living in and around this area. When I fly over their villages I begin to feel helpless because I just can't multiply myself fast enough. I keep thinking—if I just had more help. Even one more preacher . . ."

Talmadge suddenly sat up and looked Loren in the eyes. "Why don't you consider staying on here with us? Look what even two of us could do."

Loren smiled. The offer was tempting for he had grown to appreciate this man like a brother. "I'd really like to do it, Talmadge," he said. "But I can't, anymore than I can work for my aunt."

"Why not?"

"The Lord's direction has been so definite to me. Go into *all* the world and preach the Gospel," answered Loren. "I really don't understand what it means yet, Talmadge, but I know that I'm not to be here, not at this time anyway."

Talmadge's face was set. "Okay," he said quietly. "If you don't stay, then send me three others in your place!"

Loren couldn't help the laugh. "Do you really mean that?"

"Of course! I want to start a technical school for the Sengalese boys—to teach them different manual skills along with the message of the Gospel. Then they can go out into distant villages to teach more people these skills and the message of Jesus Christ . . ."

Loren raised his hands to stop him, a grin now spreading over his face. "Now there's an order I might just be able to fill. Let me tell you about a youth project that I have back home."

Loren told Talmadge the story of Youth With A Mission, and for hours the two men talked about the potential of youth in countries like Africa and other emerging nations. Even when Loren told them good-bye several days later, Talmadge was still thinking about the young people. "Don't forget, send me someone," he yelled as Loren walked toward the plane in Dakar.

"I will," Loren turned and yelled back. "I'll send someone for sure." Then he climbed into the plane to take off for South America. The engines began to rev up for takeoff. Loren looked out the window at his friends, still waving though they couldn't see him. Then the plane climbed up and away, and as it did, the present seemed to fall away with it.

Loren's mind went back to other scenes from his trip. The moment in Red Square, in Moscow, a few weeks ago. He had been standing there watching the long lines of people who wanted to see Lenin's body on display. Just then a group of Chinese visitors had come by, stopping near him to take pictures of each other with the walls of the Kremlin for background.

Loren realized that he could reach out and touch them. Yet at the same time, he was aware that a great chasm was between them. A feeling of helplessness swept over him. "How can I ever reach them in their world?" he thought. "Will anyone ever have the chance to get back into China with the Gospel?"

His mind returned to some events in Africa. He thought of a few days ago when he was flying back to Dakar from Nigeria. He looked out the window as he was doing now, but instead of blue water below him, there had been the dense green of jungle. As far as he could see, the green land was dotted with the spiraling smoke from unseen villages. Again that wave of helplessness came over him. "Who can reach these people?" he thought. "Can I reach them all in time?"

Now Loren turned from the plane window. He felt restless, like he couldn't escape something. He decided to try to rest and lay back against the seat. In that moment, the Holy Spirit condensed an experience in Nigeria to a single scene in his mind, bringing the words of his call to him once again.

It was in the village of Mberri one Sunday morning. He was

taken there by the local missionary to speak in the new church. Loren was amazed when he saw the size of the building. "It's huge!" he exclaimed and hurried inside to look around. "How did you ever get such a big church in this little village?"

"I didn't," said the missionary. "Let me tell you about the young people who did. A couple of years ago, the youth of our church in Aba, about fifty miles from here, heard about this village. It was considered a very heathen place. They became so burdened that they began to pray that this village would hear the Gospel message.

"But there seemed to be no answer. They knew that the missionaries already had more to do than time permitted. Then one of these kids suggested that maybe they should take the Gospel there themselves. So, untrained, but full of zeal, a group set out on lorries for Mberri."

The missionary took Loren to the doorway and pointed to the nearby center of the village. "When they got here, they began to go from hut to hut, telling the people about the plan of Salvation. Then they held services here in the village center every night. In three weeks time, over a thousand people had accepted the Lord. Before you knew it, they all wanted a church and wanted someone to come and teach them more of the Bible. So here it is. This is what young people can do when they put legs to their burden."

High in a plane, Africa behind him and South America ahead, Loren Cunningham had his answer. "That's it, that's it," he thought as he began digging in his briefcase for his Bible. "This is how the Great Commission can be fulfilled in my lifetime. Not by me alone, but other young people like me, going to every village and city in the world with the good news that Christ died for man's sins."

Now he saw the full potential of Youth With A Mission. It *was* to be more than a task force of Vocational Volunteers; it was to be groups of young people multiplying themselves through converts, spreading out all over the world. This was the way he could pursue his own call as well.

He must write to Talmadge right away. And he knew the very first words that he would say. "No, Talmadge, it's not impossible!"

By the time Loren got back to the United States, he was filled with plans and ideas for Youth With A Mission. But once again the official brethren of his denomination couldn't honestly share his enthusiasm. So Loren put the idea away again. After all, he reasoned, if God was directing him, then the brethren would have the same excitement about the program that he did.

He went back to recruiting for the Vocational Volunteer program. One of the recruits was a vivacious blonde, Darlene Scratch, who applied to go to Africa as a nurse. He first met her when he held a service one Sunday morning at the church her father pastored in Redwood City, California.

At dinner afterward, the conversation kept returning to Loren's work and the vision of Youth With A Mission. Later as the group was saying good-bye outside the restaurant, Loren stood for a moment alone with Darlene. "You really believe that, don't you?" she asked.

"Believe what?"

"That it's possible to reach every person on earth with the Gospel in our generation."

"Yes, I do," Loren answered.

Slowly Darlene turned and walked away. Several weeks later her application came into the YWAM office. Loren looked at it for a long time. Maybe he could talk her into making it a lifetime dedication.

And he did. They were married in June of 1963 and immediately set off on another tour of ministering in other countries. They went to Europe first where they bought a little Volkswagen to travel in. One of their first stops was at a camp of European Christians who had dedicated their vacation to an effort at literature saturation in various countries. Loren had been invited to come and join with them, since he was interested in this type of work.

One day as he and Darlene were preparing to go out door-to-door, he looked at the young people around him. It *was* possible for young people to do this kind of evangelism. He couldn't help but think of the times he had wanted to start a program like this but had held back. As he watched the young people walk out toward the village, their hands filled with Gospel literature, he suddenly knew in his heart that he had not done all that God had called him to do.

He turned to Darlene. "When we get back home, I'm going to begin announcing a witnessing outreach for next summer," he said. And he did.

By late spring of 1964, applications were coming in daily to the little office in Pasadena. It looked like there would be at least two hundred young people of Loren's denomination involved in this first outreach.

But as summer drew near, Loren noticed that something was bothering Darlene. One evening when they had a quiet moment together, he asked, "What's on your mind, Dar?"

Darlene sighed. "I'm just getting worried, I guess, about how we're going to get the money for our fares on Summer of Service. You've asked the kids to trust God and not ask for money in church services; now what about us?"

"I feel we must live by the same ideas that we ask the young people to," Loren answered slowly. "I've always felt that I should never ask for money for myself, in churches or any other way. I've always taken it as a seal upon my work when God supplied my needs."

"Yes," agreed Darlene. "It's just that time is running short and I must confess to being a little nervous about where it's going to come from."

When Loren got the answer a few days later, he could hardly wait to get back to the house and share it with Darlene. He came into his folks' home where they were staying, slamming the door with a grin.

"I got the money for our fares on SOS today!" He smiled as he kissed her.

Her eyes lit up with relief. "Wonderful! Where?"

"I got a good deal on the Volkswagen so I sold it."

"You what?" Darlene gasped. "But . . . but . . ."

She stopped for a moment. Finally she said, "Loren, that's all we've got. It's the only thing in this world that we can call our home."

Loren looked down at his bride of ten months. "I didn't know it would upset you, Dar. It honestly never occurred to me. Why, we won't need a car all summer long."

"I know," Darlene said quietly. "It just had so many wonderful memories, buying it overseas and everything. I guess it was the only thing I could hang onto."

Loren put his hands on her shoulders. "You also know, don't you, that the Lord will give us one when we need it again," he said gently.

Darlene nodded and walked to the guest bedroom where they were staying. Loren turned and went to the living-room window to look out at the street below. "I should have warned her what I had in mind," he thought. Today was the first time she had been thrown by something he did. He just hadn't thought it was important. But now he began to see what life this past year must have been like for her. Right now all their wedding presents were stored in boxes under the bed in the guest room and in the rafters of the garage. They had lived out of a suitcase since their marriage, but Darlene had been a trooper and hadn't wasted a moment complaining about it.

Maybe he should go in the bedroom now and share the Scripture that God gave him after he sold everything to go to Bible college. *"I tell you this, there is no one who has given up home, or wife, brothers, parents, or children, for the sake of the Kingdom of God, who will not be repaid many times over in this age, and in the age to come have eternal life"* (Luke 18:29 NEB).

Loren went to the bedroom and opened the door softly. Darlene was on her knees in prayer. He shut the door again. The Lord was taking care of the matter better than he could. He was just glad that the problem of giving up things had gone out of his life at nineteen so he wouldn't have to face a situation like that again.

In the hectic weeks of preparation that followed, Loren saw that Darlene had received an answer, for she faced the summer with a peace amid the chaos of preparing menus, literature, first-aid kits, and other necessary items.

The first Summer of Service in 1964 was outstanding. Loren learned many concepts through experiences with teams in the Bahamas and Dominican Republic which would become the foundation for future outreaches. He learned that Satan could use human frailties to advantage when Christians stepped out boldly to reach a country with the news of Jesus Christ. Some of the lessons came through mistakes. Others came through the successes. There were teams of young people working on nearly all populated islands in the Bahamas. Spanish-speaking teams went to the Dominican Republic. Both groups saw miracles of healing, of God's provision for water and sometimes for food when something happened to their supply. They learned the power of prayer when Communist agitators began to stir up a crowd of thousands at a street service. God intervened in the situation and none of the group was hurt when the agitators began to throw rocks.

One night in late August, Loren and Darlene had a moment alone to review the summer. "Hasn't it been something to see these hundreds of people make decisions for Christ?" Darlene asked happily.

"Yes," smiled Loren. "My moment comes when I see the kids walking back in the afternoon, their bodies sagging wearily but their faces shining with eagernesss to share what they've experienced that day. That's when it seems like the dream of kids spreading out all over the world isn't a dream any longer, it's a reality."

But within a few weeks, they wondered if the kids would ever have another chance. Loren received word from his headquarters to come and meet with the executive brethren again.

They arrived in the headquarters' city in early December. "I'm afraid I'm in for some tough going this time," Loren told Darlene as he left her off at a motel.

"Why?"

"Let's face it. Our program goes against the established procedures for missions, you know, not requiring Bible school training and all that."

"Well," Darlene said, "at least now they have an example of what you have in mind so that the program can be accepted or rejected on its own merits."

"Yeah," Loren smiled as he kissed her good-bye.

It was late afternoon when he got back to the motel. "Well?" said Darlene, looking at him anxiously. Loren sank wearily into a chair, wondering how to tell her about it, whether to give it to her straight or break it gently.

"I'm not sure," he said finally. "At first nothing too definite was actually said. Everyone was kind to me and . . ."

"But what about Youth With A Mission?"

Loren took a deep breath, trying to remember the conversations exactly. "It seemed like the consensus was that the program just isn't right for our denominational orgaization."

"I see," she said quietly. "And?"

Loren knew he couldn't hold anything from her. Somehow she sensed he had more to say. Slowly he stood up and walked over to look out the window.

"There is something else," he began. "I was talking with a couple of the men later. I guess I was continuing to press my case because I got to saying that I felt there was a new generation coming up that was completely different from all the rest. Then I said that unless we gave them a bigger challenge than what they've had in the past, we would lose them."

Now Darlene came over to look at him. "What did they say to that?"

Loren turned to face her. "One of the men said that if I didn't follow the wishes of the brethren, I would be embarrassed nationally."

"What did he mean?"

"It seems to me that he meant I would lose my ministerial standing," he answered as gently as he could.

Darlene's face went white.

"Darlene, when they said that, something inside just took over. I couldn't help myself. I heard my voice saying, Well, let's pray. They suggested that I was the one who should pray, so I just did. The words came out, I couldn't hold them back."

"What did you pray?" whispered Darlene.

"I remember praying, 'Lord, break me at the foot of the cross. I want Your will no matter what.' "

V

"When you don't have a denomination, where do you preach and who are your friends?" asked Darlene.

Loren looked at the road ahead. "I don't know. The thought had never occurred to me—until this last week."

They were driving west along the highway out of Dallas Texas. The last couple of days had been like a strange dream. They came as far as Dallas where Loren preached on Sunday. As they were getting ready to leave on Monday morning, the motor blew in the microbus that they were driving. They had bought the secondhand bus in Miami to haul teams back up the east coast after SOS. In a way, Loren was kind of glad for the breakdown, for it gave him something to think about instead of the headquarters' encounter.

But now, with the engine fixed, he was glad to be back on the highway. It meant that they would have to drive all night tonight because of the two-day delay, but he wasn't worried. He had driven many a night before. Besides, he felt ready now to resume the discussion of his future with Darlene, now that his mind was clearer for action.

"Ever since last Friday," he said, "it's like I'm looking at a puzzle from a whole new angle. Up to now I had just taken for granted that God's will in my life would work in conjunction with my denomination. I guess it was because I grew up in it and all; I just assumed it was my birthright."

"I know," Darlene said.

Loren looked over at her. He hadn't thought about it before, but she was giving up her church heritage, too. He wondered what her father would say. And what his own father, an officer in the denomination, would say about this turn of events.

"The hardest part," he said aloud, "is going to be telling our folks."

Darlene took a deep breath. "Yes."

Loren turned his attention back to the highway. They had

fallen into another one of those deep lapses which had characterized their existence the last five days. His mind went back to the moment he had knelt before the presbyters of his district, as they laid hands on him, praying the prayer of ordination.

"If I lose my ordination, I won't be able to recruit young people in our churches," he said now. "What can I do and how can I preach if I have no credentials?"

Darlene sat quiet a moment. "You could teach. You have a degree and everything. And I could go back into nursing again. That would give us the finances to spend our summers doing this work, if you feel that is what God wants us to do."

"Yes, but what missionaries do you work with on the field?" he said aloud while his mind jumped back to the fellowship he had enjoyed in his previous travels. From deep in his heart a protest silently cried out, "But these are my brothers!"

All through the night the battle raged within Loren. There didn't seem to be any answers or reasons for all this.

The light of morning began to bring the desert into form. He was finally really tired enough both physically and mentally to sleep well. It seemed like he had been asking himself questions and working out answers for hours. "I don't understand what is happening, Lord," he prayed, "but I know I can't turn my back on Your call in my life."

Darlene began to stir from her sleep in the back seat. "Would you like to stop for some breakfast?" she said, rubbing her eyes. "Then I could drive."

"Uh huh," Loren nodded, already feeling the tension beginning to ease from his arms. "There should be something up ahead in Tucson."

After breakfast he crawled into the sleeping bag on the back seat. He zipped it up halfway, and stretched out, enjoying the sensation of being too tired to have to work at going to sleep. He lay there a minute, looking at the sun catch the light on Darlene's hair. "Bless her," he thought. "She's being a trooper again." He knew she disliked driving this awkward bus but she was having a go at it anyway.

He drifted off into a deep sleep, the first one he had known for days. Hours later, far away in his dark sleep, he heard Darlene calling. He tried to force his senses awake, but they would not respond. Something was wrong and he couldn't wake up fast enough. He heard her again.

"Loren, Loren, I'm losing control!" she was calling.

The microbus was bouncing radically. "A tire has blown," he thought. "I must sit up and help her . . ." Just then he felt the car hit the soft sand of the road shoulder. It began rocking crazily and then turned over, going into a roll. There came an awful sound of shattering glass as the sides, then the roof, hit the ground. He was halfway through a window now, and could feel the pavement against his body. The car was still rolling.

"If I don't get back I'll be crushed next time," he thought and pushed against the pavement with every ounce of strength that he had. The car began its second roll and that was all he remembered for a moment of time.

When he came to, the car was rolling over another time. The big side doors had swung open and he was being thrown out, still partly in the sleeping bag. He lay stunned in the sand as all grew quiet around him. Then he sat up slowly and tried to get his bearings. He found that blood was streaming down his face. He looked over at the microbus and could see it was demolished. Then he remembered his wife.

"Darlene, Darlene!" he called.

There was no answer. Just the awesome silence of the desert. He looked around and then he saw her, lying face down in the sand with a suitcase on top of her. He crawled over as fast as he could, calling to her as he went. But she didn't move.

Gently he lifted the suitcase off. On the back of her head was one of the ugliest gashes that he had ever seen. Quickly he turned her over, taking her in his arms. As he did, strange guttural sounds, like an eerie sigh, came from her throat. Her eyes were glassy and rolled back. She wasn't breathing.

"Don't die, please don't die." He was saying it over and over as the blood from the cut on his head splashed down onto her face. And in that moment Loren heard the voice of God again.

"Loren, do you still want to serve Me?" came the words to his heart.

Loren looked around him. All he could see was the wrecked car and beyond that their luggage, clothing—everything they had—strewn about in the sand. There was nothing else but the desert. Not a house or a car in sight. Just miles and miles of silent desert under a burning sun.

Slowly Loren lifted up his head. "God, I don't have anything left but You," he said simply. "No matter what the cost, I want to serve You and You alone. My trust is in You now and my life is still in Your hands."

Suddenly, more words came in answer. "Pray for Darlene."

Loren looked down at her. There wasn't a movement or flicker of life. But God had told him to pray, so he did. Minutes passed. He thought he saw her trying to gasp for air. Then he realized he was trying to breathe for her and knew even as he did that it was useless. If life returned, it would come from God.

A car stopped out on the road. The driver, a Mexican man, came and said he would go for help, but it might be a long wait. They were almost to Ajo, near the Mexican border. As he watched the man drive off, Loren realized that Darlene must have taken the wrong turn in Gila Bend.

A few minutes later a camper truck stopped. The men, dressed for hunting, came over and looked at the scene silently. "Look, mister," one said finally. "She's about to die. There's a military base near here and they may have a doctor. We can take you in the camper."

Loren hovered over her as they drove down the road. But there was no doctor at the base. They turned to leave when the ambulance from town arrived. Darlene was carefully lifted inside and they drove off, sirens screaming.

There was no room in the back, so Loren sat with two men in front, reaching back to hold her hand. It was going to be a long ride. The nearest hospital was in Phoenix, eighty miles away. Loren kept turning to watch Darlene. It seemed like she was breathing in a way, but each breath seemed to be a fierce battle. They had gone about forty miles when Loren heard God speak to him again. "She is going to be all right."

Just then Darlene raised up slightly and opened her eyes. They were clear and she smiled at him for just a second, then lay back down.

She never remembered the moment. She continued to be unconscious for several hours while they x-rayed her in the hospital. They made Loren lie down too, in another room. It wasn't until then that he remembered he had been in the wreck, too. There were great marks on his legs where the zipper of the sleeping bag had gouged him. And he had a back injury which meant he would have to wear a brace for a year or so.

"But otherwise," smiled the doctor as he finished bandaging his head, "you're in pretty good condition."

Later Loren lay on a stretcher, talking to his father who had phoned from Los Angeles. His dad was just asking about Darlene when a nurse hurried up. "Your wife is awake and calling for you," she said. Then she smiled. "She's going to make it now."

The local pastor took Loren into his home for a few days, so that he could get to the hospital easily to see Darlene. Saturday morning he went to see her as usual.

"Now my day can start with you here," she smiled from the bed. They hadn't known for sure whether her back was broken until they had developed the X rays. They showed no break, but the ligaments were so torn, and the back so bruised, that the doctors warned it would remain painfully swollen for many months to come.

Loren took her hand. "I'm still scheduled to speak in Los Angeles tomorrow," he said gently. "If I'm going to cancel out I'll have to phone them right away."

Darlene lay quietly for a long moment. "You know that I'm going to be here a long time recuperating," she said finally. "It won't be a matter of days, but of weeks and months before I'm up to traveling around again." She paused now, but Loren held back. He knew it would have to be her decision. "Aren't you supposed to go on to New York and speak at some churches and at Teen Challenge?"

Loren nodded. "It'll be at least a month before I can see you again."

Darlene rested a moment. "I know," she said. "But I'm well taken care of here and my folks want to fly me to Redwood City as soon as I can be moved, so that they can take care of me. And my friends will be coming by to see me," she smiled. "It won't be as lonely as it sounds."

Loren looked at her, wondering if she was just saying it to make him feel better.

"After all," she went on, "we don't know how long these churches will be open to us."

Loren squeezed her hand. "It's in God's hands now, Sweetheart."

"Yes," said Darlene, her face growing serious. "And so are you and so am I. Loren, if you stay here because I want you to, it will be because we don't trust God enough to take care of us."

Loren nodded, a smile growing inside him. Darlene took another deep breath. "Perhaps the Lord wants us to learn how to live together, though separate," she mused. "Well, I'll begin now by promising to pray for you every time I think of you."

Loren bent over and put his arms around her the best he could. As he kissed her good-bye suddenly all the rational thoughts left him and his only desire was to carry her away gently to some nice, warm place where she could recover peacefully and they could be together.

Later, as he walked down the corridor, he realized that if he gave up Darlene a thousand times, it would never become easy.

VI

In New York, Loren stayed at the first building of the Teen Challenge Center. He was up on the top floor in a room starkly furnished with a bed and cabinet. It was cold outside, snow and ice everywhere, which discouraged unnecessary travel. So he had many hours alone in which to think and pray. He began to relive the events leading up to the desert.

Over and over again he would return to one concept. Jesus Christ was Lord. And if He was to be Lord of a life, then everything else must take second place. If he wasn't willing to live his life as a sacrifice unto God, then how dare he ask anyone else to take a step to serve Christ? His mind would go back to the many people he had witnessed to in countries where it would sometimes mean death to be a Christian.

"And what about all those conversions last summer?" he thought. "If I were to go back today, how many would still be following Christ?"

In the midst of his pondering on his last day there, a knock came at the door and Watson Argue, Jr., came into the room. It had been in his church that Loren had spoken that first Sunday after the wreck. J.R. was a special friend. Not only had he been best man at Loren's wedding, but he also served on the Youth With A Mission board. Right now he was in the east, setting up some crusade meetings for an evangelist.

"Well, how are you getting along?" J.R. grinned.

Loren paused before answering. He knew he needed to talk out his thinking with someone so he decided to share his thoughts with him. "I've really been questioning some things deeply and I need some answers."

"What kind of answers?"

"Well, I've really been questioning things about salvation," Loren began. "Like what really is the cost of salvation? Do converts truly give their lives to Christ and are we making it clear that they should?"

Loren was dead serious but he noticed that Watson had a twinkle in his eye. He decided to explain further. "I keep thinking of those converts last summer. We had over three thousand recorded in the Bahamas and twenty-five hundred in the Dominican Republic. But what really took place? Is it enough to ask them to believe that Jesus died for them, lead them in the sinner's prayer, and give them some Scripture verses?"

The twinkle in J.R.'s eye had spread to a grin on his face. "You know who you need to talk to? A man I met last week. His name is Harry Conn."

"Who's he?" Loren asked.

"I met him back in Rockford, Illinois. He has things really straight and logical about salvation and has light on it that I had never seen before."

"Is he a preacher?"

"No, he's a businessman. In fact, he's president of the company. You should have seen him. All he could talk about was spiritual things."

"What's his denomination?" said Loren.

J.R. broke into a laugh. "Oh, I don't know. And it won't matter when you meet him. Wait and see. The day I met him, we were talking in his office. It's enclosed with glass so all the factory workers can see him. But he didn't care. Sometimes tears would course down his cheeks as he would share some insight into Scripture. He had his Bible open there and was turning from Scripture to Scripture. I just couldn't get over his dedication and enthusiasm."

Loren sat thinking. He was leaving for California this very afternoon. Maybe he could stop and see this man. "Look, J.R., would you mind calling him?"

"No, come on. I'll introduce you on the phone."

They climbed down the stairs to the phone in the bottom hall. Watson told Mr. Conn about Loren and then handed him the receiver.

"Hello, Mr. Conn," said Loren. "I would like to come and talk with you sometime. Watson tells me that you might have something that will help me."

"Well, brother," came a voice booming back. "I'm supposed to speak at an engineering meeting up in Wisconsin tonight but I think God wants me to talk to you instead. I'll cancel out the meeting."

Now Loren was embarrassed. "Oh, don't do that. I'm on my way back to California but I'll be back in the Chicago area sometime. Maybe I can see you then."

"Nope!" came the man's voice. "I tell you, I will meet you today. Just take the Rockford bus from the airport and I'll meet you in front of the hotel where it stops."

It was just a matter of hours before Loren was standing at the bus stop, waiting for this stranger who had suddenly popped into his life. A car drove up and Harry Conn got out and introduced himself. No sooner had Loren gotten settled in the car than Harry started talking.

"First of all, we should talk about the reality and necessity of true repentance," he began.

"He is really just like J.R. said!" thought Loren.

"Now you see, true repentance means submission to the rule and reign of Jesus Christ in the heart of a man," said Harry.

"Yes," nodded Loren, remembering his thinking that very morning.

"It is the setting up of the Moral Government of God within a life."

"Moral Government?" thought Loren. That was something new. "What do you mean, Moral Government," he asked.

"Well, back in the great revivals on the college campuses of America in the 1800's, the kids began to refer to the term 'Kingdom of God' as the 'Moral Government of God,' to make it clearer to the understanding of modern man."

They drove up to Harry's house and went inside with Loren still listening and asking questions. After supper Conn brought out notes and charts that he had made on the subject.

"We were made to worship God, Loren," cried Harry, at one point. "When the Lord withdrew himself from man's presence back in the Garden of Eden, a mighty void developed in man's personality. Look at man today. He is still trying to fill that void with money, prestige, security, religion—oh, any number of things. But that void is a God-sized one, and only He can fill it!"

The more Harry talked, the more excited Loren became. It was like a light inside was slowly warming up, becoming brighter and brighter. "Why this is the same thing I used to hear my grandfathers preach," he thought. "Salvation isn't the blind leap of faith as I've heard it described in recent years. It is a logical, sensible step that man should take."

Loren settled back in his chair and for several hours the two men talked, checking their ideas with scriptural teaching. It was very late when Loren finally got on a plane for San Francisco, but he wasn't tired.

From that day on, Loren felt that he had been given a new key, one that opened doors where he had never thought to venture before. His inward life seemed turned in a different direction, not to the left or right, but straight up. He met new people all the time, and each one seemed to add to his spiritual growth and learning, some without even being aware of it.

Without hesitation he began announcing the 1965 Summer of Service everywhere he went. Now he was ministering in churches of various denominations. His fears that the movement would be stunted proved groundless. He and Darlene were busier than before. It was as if walls surrounding him had been lifted and he had new eyes to see the body of Jesus Christ.

Whenever possible, he would expose the kids on the YWAM teams to the same kind of concepts by bringing some of his teachers in to lecture them during orientation times on crusades. Sometimes observers would criticize, pointing out that these men were so deep in teaching, young people could never grasp it. Loren just smiled. It took a year or two to prove his reasons; then it became plain. The young people were beginning to flourish in all that spiritual light and were taking giant steps in following after God.

VII

It was near the end of Summer of Service in 1966 that Loren saw that YWAM was expanding too fast for him to keep up. Now full-time leadership was needed for the various areas of outreach.

"But I feel that I can't ask someone to come full time," he said to Darlene one night. "We have nothing to offer them financially. They would have to live the same life of faith that we do."

Darlene just looked up and said, "God has always supplied our needs; can't He do the same thing in filling this need for a staff?"

Loren smiled in spite of himself. And that night they committed this new need to the Lord. They decided to say nothing about it but to trust God to raise up the right people for the job.

Within days, a young man from Canada, Arnold Breit-kreuz, came to Loren before the teams went home from Jamaica. "I feel God is leading me into working with Youth With A Mission full time," he said. And from that conversation developed a full-time outreach all across the country of Canada.

A few days later, the directors of the Latin American SOS, Wedge and Shirley Alman, came up to Loren. They, too, felt called by God to join YWAM full time even though it meant giving up the pastorate of a church they had pioneered.

Another team member in the Caribbean in 1966 was Floyd McClung. During 1967 he married Y-wammer Sally Claiborn, who was working as the secretary in the YWAM office. They felt the call of God to go full time and Floyd was able to direct the Caribbean outreach.

At the end of Summer of Service in 1966, two Y-wammers, Jim Rogers and Janice Cunningham, got married. They had been on all three Summer of Service crusades. Jim held the special distinction of being the first young person to sell his horse in order to go. Jan was very special to Loren too, for she was his younger sister. The day of the wedding Jim came to Loren.

"The Lord has been dealing with me about going on YWAM full time," he said.

It was Jim and Jan who went with Loren the following January to New Zealand to begin another Youth With A Mission outreach. Darlene stayed at home.

"I can go back to work as a nurse," she volunteered cheerfully when she saw that there wasn't enough money for both of them to go. "It will give me something to do and help take care of our finances."

Loren was hesitant until the Lord made it very clear that this was His time for him to step out. When he got to New Zealand, Jim and Jan and several others from the United States were already there. He found out that some people who heard him speak in the United States had recommended him so he was scheduled to start immediately at a conference on Great Barrier Island. It was during this time that he met Jim and Joy Dawson. In talks with them he began to learn new insights into the area of the power of prayer and the Holy Spirit's leading in a life. During the conference he announced that the first YWAM door-to-door witnessing crusade in New Zealand would take place in Auckland, beginning a week from Saturday.

At the end of the conference Loren didn't know what to do next. He knew that he must get into churches to recruit the young people. But at that moment, he had no definite place to start and no place to stay in Auckland. Jim and Joy came up to him during this time and told him that they felt the Lord impressing them to invite him to stay in their "prophet's chamber." Loren accepted eagerly for he wanted to learn more from this couple.

But when he got to the room in Auckland, the Lord spoke to him, directing him to go into a fast.

"But what about the crusade?" argued Loren in his mind. "I've got to spread the word and recruit kids or it will be a flop."

The answer which came to his mind was, "When you are weak, then are you strong."

So Loren spent the week alone before God, letting Him turn on the searchlight of truth into his heart. It meant dying to his desires for a successful crusade. And it also meant writing several letters of restitution as God the Father gently brought into the light certain things and attitudes which Loren had hidden from himself.

Saturday morning Loren walked into the church for the beginning of the first New Zealand outreach. Fifty-five young people with eager faces were waiting for him. *"Not by might, nor by power, but by my spirit, saith the Lord"* (Zechariah 4:6) rang over and over inside him as he walked to the front.

It was in this crusade that Loren saw that YWAM had truly become a movement of young people from many different denominations. More and more he was discovering there was a spiritual awakening occurring among Christians of all faiths. Young people everywhere, not just in the United States, were looking for some way to do a work for God.

By the end of the first five months in New Zealand, a total of 215 young people had participated in door-to-door witnessing crusades. Some of the group formed a pilot team and went to Fiji, the Hebrides, and New Caledonia.

When Loren got back home, he and Darlene began to share some of the things they had learned from God while apart. They were more than slightly amazed to find that the very things God had dealt with Loren about were what He also brought to Darlene's heart. They compared notes. The time was the same week that Loren was called into a fast.

One of the young people on the first New Zealand crusade was a young man from the Tongan Islands named Kalafi

Moala. When he saw the potential of the group, he invited them to conduct a Summer of Service in Tonga. The teams arrived in time for the coronation of King Taufa'ahau on July 4, 1967. During the days prior to the ceremony, the streets of the main city were filled night and day with Tongans and visitors. So the teams held open-air meetings almost continuously and watched in amazement as their supply of gospel literature went down so low that they had to ration it out the rest of the summer.

Loren was involved in some of the other SOS crusades in 1967 so he was unable to see the one in Tonga in action. Yet it was from this crusade that he began to see the harvest of God's leading in the past.

Tonga received the Gospel for the first time from devout Protestant missionaries, as was the case in other South Pacific kingdoms. But through the years, what began as a remarkable move of God, slowly became a form of religion and a way of life to the people. True repentance was no longer preached, and the country closed its doors to missionaries from some other denominations which still preached this kind of Gospel. But the YWAM teams didn't represent any one denomination, so they were invited into the land.

Loren read the reports that Jim and Jan sent him from Tonga. It proved to be one of the most exciting crusades ever conducted. There were many hundreds of conversions and an exciting movement of the Holy Spirit among the young people of the Kingdom. Often it was leaders and even pastors who came forward to give their lives to Christ at the end of a service.

"I've preached about sin week after week for fifteen years," said one pastor as he came forward first in an altar call. "But every week I went out of the church the same way—disobedient to God; and so did my people."

It was after this crusade that Loren saw how perfect God's plan had been when he was forced to give up his denominational ties. This movement of young people couldn't have fit into God's Kingdom any other way. Because members of the teams were from all kinds of Christian backgrounds, it meant that the only way they could work together and accomplish anything was in the name and for the sake of Jesus Christ.

By the summer of 1968 the Summer of Service branched out even further. There were three separate outreaches in the Caribbean all summer. Teams worked in three Central American countries. A unique in-depth literature saturation and witnessing crusade was conducted in the Canadian province of Quebec. Another new phase of SOS was begun with the Trans/USA team which worked in United States' cities.

That summer brought another dimension to the lives of Loren and Darlene. Their first child, Karen Joy, was born in the early morning hours of July 4th with Loren just making it back to California in time from the Trans/USA crusade in New York.

At the end of summer, Jim and Carole Carmichael from California felt led to stay on the East Coast and set up some sort of permanent witnessing outreach. The same day, while they were praying about the decision, a large plot of ground was donated to YWAM to be used as a headquarters' office for the East and a supply depot for literature and materials.

In the fall, Jim and Jan Rogers headed up the first Around The World team. It was made up of young people from Canada, United States, and New Zealand. They spent their time in various countries, training national young people in personal evangelism. The team finished their year in August of 1969 in Kenya, Africa. From there Jim and Jan flew to Europe and met Darlene and Loren who were working with a team in Kitzingen, Germany.

It was the first time they had seen each other in sixteen months. So even though it was 2 a.m. when Jim and Jan got to the home where Loren and Darlene were staying, the four stayed up talking.

"First," smiled Jan, "let me tell you how God used Joy Dawson to help us in a special way. . ."

Loren smiled at Darlene. It almost sounded like his report back to her in 1967. He settled back in the chair to listen.

"When we went to Fiji in 1968 to work in the SOS there, we were feeling very empty, really in need of help in our spiritual ministry. When we'd pray about this, Joy Dawson would come to our minds, like she was to be the one to help us.

"After SOS we were just in New Zealand a few days, for we felt the Lord was leading us to go to Australia and begin another YWAM outreach there. Friday was our last day before taking off, and we were really beginning to think that maybe we'd been off the track on this Joy Dawson business when the phone rang. She was inviting us to dinner!"

"But Janie had determined not to bring up the subject," said Jim. "So all evening long, not a word was said about how she got leading or guidance from God. Finally we stood up to have prayer just before we left. Afterward Joy said, 'I have just asked God to tell me if there are any other purposes He wants to fulfill. He has said "Share with them your methods of daily Bible reading and Bible study." So I'm going to open up my "kit of tools" for you. The Lord has impressed upon me that your greatest need at this time is for the Word of God to have a far more vital place in your daily lives and that your effectiveness in future service depends upon this.' "

"Well, I just couldn't help the tears," said Jan. "It was exactly the help that we were praying for. So when we got over to Sydney to start YWAM there, we found that her help was just what we needed in finding the Lord's guidance on matters instead of leaning to our own ideas and plans.

"You should have seen it in Australia," Jan continued. "You know that Kalafi and his wife Tapu were there already going to school. So they met us. Before the end of that very first day, God opened up a brand-new office for us to use. Every morning, instead of bustling into the office and starting on phone calls to the list of contacts we had, the four of us would go before God in prayer to seek guidance for that particular day. Then we would just stand back in amazement at the way God opened doors for us."

"Even in the sphere of leadership," Jim said. "God met the need in a complete way. You remember when we were ready to come home from New Zealand in 1968 that Ross Tooley and Dean Sherman were able to take over the leadership."

Both Loren and Darlene smiled now, remembering the way Dean had come to work in the Southern Hemisphere. He came from the United States to participate in the Tongan SOS. Afterward he felt constrained to stay on and work in New Zealand. He landed there at the end of their winter season with just one suitcase filled with lightweight tropical clothing.

"Anyway," Jim continued, "when we saw that God was leading us on the Around the World team, Dean was already over in Sydney with us. So again he was able to continue the outreach there while Ross took over the full load in New Zealand."

Now Darlene leaned forward. "Before you go on, bring us up to date on Kalafi."

"They're making plans right now to go into New Guinea and start a YWAM outreach there," said Jim. "Also, our last report from him said that the work in Tonga is continuing. His sister is heading up a correspondence-course program as well as opening up a literature center."

The room fell silent a moment, each one lost in his own thoughts.

Then Darlene sat up straight. "Jan, you've got to tell us about Around The World before we all fall asleep!"

Jan laughed. "You and Loren probably told us something about Indonesia when you came back from there, but I just wasn't prepared for the place."

"What do you mean?" Loren asked.

"Oh, it was just so foreign. I guess it was because we had worked in mostly English-speaking areas before. I remember the first night there. We were in this little hotel in Djakarta. It was so hot at 2 a.m. that I couldn't sleep. So I stood out on the balcony. I was amazed to see that there was a stream of humanity going past. Peddlers shouting their wares, betja drivers in their pedal cabs, people on their way to market."

"It was a good place to break in for working in Southeast Asia," Jim observed. "At first, the local young people were really nervous about going door-to-door in Moslem neighborhoods. Our kids from the United States and New Zealand would encourage them, though, and soon the group grew to about forty-five Indonesians witnessing with us."

"We found this true in many countries," added Jan. "But when the kids saw the power of the Gospel to change lives, they weren't afraid anymore. It was in Indonesia that we came face-to-face with Moslems, Buddhists, Hindus, and even Communists and learned how to deal with each one."

Loren and Dar sat quietly as Jim and Jan continued to tell of their adventures. The team spent two months in the Philippines, working on the university campus one month, and another month traveling in boats and even living on an outrigger, in order to reach people on remote islands. In Thailand they walked for miles under a burning sun, up in a remote province which never received a Gospel witness before. In India they worked in the city of Calcutta during May, one of the hottest and most humid months.

"These last two months in Africa have really been exciting," said Jan. "Just before we left, we were the morning Bible teachers to four hundred kids at a youth camp. We gave them training in personal witnessing, and at the end of the week, they took us in buses to the city of Kisumu so we could saturate it with a Gospel witness."

Now Jim leaned forward, his face sober. "We're really going to have to pray for those kids," he said. "You probably heard that one of the national leaders, Tom Mboya, was assassinated a couple of weeks ago."

Loren nodded.

"Well, the tension is really building up now between the Luo tribe to which Mboya belonged and the Kikuyu tribe."

"Didn't the Mau Mau come from the Kikuyu tribe?" asked Loren.

"Yes," said Jim. "And the kids told us that they heard that some of the Kikuyu were demanding that the people take loyalty oaths again. Some of the young people who went witnessing with us last week are Kikuyu. Now they're wondering if they will have to choose between taking the oath or dying for their belief in Christ."

Darlene spoke. "Let me tell you about our hosts here at this house," she said quietly. "You'll meet them in the morning. After the war they escaped from Poland into East Germany. Then, after some time there, they were finally able to escape once again.

"The other day our YWAM kids felt they were doing too much for all of us and began to protest against all their kindness. They just said, 'We lost everything in the War. Then we lost it again when we left Poland. And we lost it all again when we left East Germany. We know we have it for only a short time and we want to share it in order to get the Gospel out."

The room went quiet. Loren looked across at his sister and her husband. "They aren't kids anymore," he thought. "They've faced up to the same responsibility that I had to in New York four years ago. It's not a cute game that we're playing. We're in a deadly serious business of winning the world to Christ and it's going to cost us everything we've got."

VIII

A week after Loren's visit with Jim and Jan, Summer of Service, 1969, came to a close. Teams began to trek back to various debriefing headquarters. The European teams met in a little hotel in the foothills of Switzerland.

Loren stood watching another dust-covered vehicle make its way up the hill toward the hotel, kids and luggage jammed every which way. He didn't know which was the most exciting. Moving out with the kids at the beginning of the summer, each team member an unknown quantity, or this moment of reunion. Now the kids were piling out of the vehicle, squealing and yelling as they saw their friends. Everyone was telling of his summer adventures faster than they could be heard. The team from Paris, France, was the last to arrive. Some had driven all the way up from Malaga, Spain. Others came in from Holland, Germany, and Austria.

"We can spend the whole day tomorrow listening to each person give a brief report of his summer," thought Loren. Then his mind jumped ahead to the next week. He and Darlene and the baby would fly to Kenosha, Wisconsin, and meet with the leaders and some of the Y-wammers from the areas of the Caribbean, Latin America, United States, and Canada. Maybe on the way to the United States they could stop off in London long enough to see Peter Stenhouse and the other four members of the ATW team who felt led to stay on there and begin a permanent outreach for Great Britain.

It would be good to see everyone again, he realized, as the faces of the staff came before him. How special each one was to him! A real friend in the truest sense of the word. There was a special bond between him and each of them. No, it didn't stop there. "Let's face it," he thought. "That same bond exists between missionaries, pastors—every child of God I've met around the world."

In the midst of his musing, he glanced at his watch. He'd better see how the kids were doing in the kitchen and round up everyone else for dinner.

The young people gathered in a glassed-in dining room for their first meal together since May. They were all standing by their chairs, waiting for the blessing on the meal, when someone began to sing. *"Praise God from whom all blessings flow..."* Everyone joined in and as they sang, Loren felt a joy rise up within him. He sensed that everyone else was feeling it, too. *"Praise Him all creatures here below..."* It rose like a great tide within the room, pushing against the walls.

He had experienced it before and learned to recognize that this joy always came after times of complete obedience to the voice of the Lord. Now everyone in the room was knowing the same sensation. He was glad. They would have many kinds of rewards for the summer. Some of it would be the awe of their friends and, in some cases, the adulation of church people. But he knew that none of it would satisfy them like this moment.

By the end of the debriefing conference, the widow who owned the hotel signed a lease agreement which meant the School of Evangelism could headquarter there during the following winter. This was the second term of the school. Loren conducted the first one during the spring and summer of 1969. New students for the second term came in June of 1969 to work on SOS and then spend the fall in language study.

The School of Evangelism was very special to Loren. Here at last was a place where young people could gather together for six months or a year and pursue the methods of evangelism. Now the many men and women who had been teachers to Loren these past years could come for one-and two-week seminars, spending hour after hour with the eager young people, sharing their insights into the work of the

Lord. During these seminars Loren listened right along with the students. Every time he heard these people speak, there was something new for him to learn.

Early in the spring of 1970, one of the speakers was the man known as Brother Andrew. He had dedicated his life to taking the Bible into Communist countries. One day Loren sat listening to Brother Andrew talk with that enthusiasm which marks a man happy with his life. As Loren looked at the faces of the students around him, he saw that they, too. were infected with his excitement in serving God.   Dan Ivanovich was sitting there, every muscle tensed, trying to absorb all that the man was saying about Russia.

"And now," Brother Andrew went on, "I would like to share with you something which has developed since the book about my work was written."

The room became absolutely still, every eye on his face. "During the last two years, Albania has set about to eradicate Christianity from their country. They have destroyed churches and taken the lives of many Christians."

As Loren heard the words, every nerve inside him suddenly came alive and a chill went down his spine. For at that moment he suddenly remembered a dream he had in 1961. He had never considered it important so he never told anyone about it. But now, he was remembering and with the remembering was coming a quickening in his heart, like when God was speaking to him.

In his dream, he drove up to a border of a foreign country and got out of a vehicle. There were other vehicles with him, but the thing that he remembered, that stayed with him the next day, was that this was the border of Albania. How clearly he remembered how the ground looked, how deep blue the sky was. He walked up to the border guard, showed his passport and was waved on to enter the country. Waiting for him on the other side was a bus. He boarded it with the rest of the people and it drove off into the country. That was all of the dream he remembered now, for the only reason he had even given it any thought the next day was that Albania was closed to the outside world.

Brother Andrew was continuing to speak. "The body of Christ is going to have to minister in Albania by coming in from the outside. It will have to be a person-to-person ministry for there are no Bibles even printed in their language at the present time."

After Brother Andrew finished the session, Loren steered him to a quiet corner. "Tell me more about Albania," he said.

"You know, Loren," Brother Andrew mused, "these young people might be the perfect answer to minister there. There is talk that Albania may soon open its borders to tourists."

Loren leaned forward in his chair; that chill had run down his spine again. "We drive down that way every year when the students go to the Holy Land to study the life of Christ."

Brother Andrew grinned. "There is just one hitch though," he said. "They don't allow you to drive in the country. When you get to the border, you must leave your vehicle there and take buses into the land."

"I know," said Loren softly, for a lump had risen in his throat. Carefully he cleared his throat. "Brother Andrew, I had a dream nine years ago. I'd like to tell you about it."

Later that day, Loren finally had a moment to talk with Darlene in their room. Karen was playing contentedly on the floor as the two moved over by the window. Loren was about to speak when Darlene laid her hand on his arm. "I've been wanting to tell you that I realize what is going on in your mind," she said quietly.

Loren looked at her in amazement as she continued. "One of your principles has been that you never would challenge anyone else to do something that you weren't willing to do yourself."

Loren nodded.

"Even though," she went on, "that may mean risking your life to minister in an Iron Curtain country. I just want you to know that I am with you on it." Loren turned from her face, serene and calm in the twilight, and looked out the window for a long moment. The Alps were growing dim in the distance and suddenly the world outside seemed cold and dark except for the lights on the snow from the School of Evangelism windows.

"I had a dream nine years ago," he said slowly. "A dream I

never told anyone about until today because I didn't think it was important." He told her about it then, and about his conversation with Brother Andrew. When he finished he stood there, waiting for her to respond. Then he remembered. He remembered another dream, one that Darlene had told him. He knew without looking at her that she was remembering the same thing... that morning when she had stood before him saying, "I dreamt last night that you were separated from me, off in another country. We were cut off. There was no way that I could find out if you were alive. It seemed like months or years . . ."

"Well, you know that most dreams don't come true, Sweetheart," he had said lightly, brushing it aside. But now, he turned to look at Darlene's face. She stood looking up at him with the same tranquil peace on her features that had been there moments before. Some time in the last seven years, she had made the same commitment that he made on the desert six years ago.

Outside in the hall, someone called that supper was ready. Loren went over to Karen who was still playing on the floor. He picked her up with one hand, taking Darlene's hand in the other. There were so many things that he wanted to tell his wife at that moment; about what she meant to him; about how happy he was to be called by God to serve Him; about how full and complete he felt seeing God fulfill a calling through his life and the lives of thousands of other young people.

But he couldn't speak. For just then, the words of Jesus Christ came into his mind. "Whoever cares for his own safety is lost; but if a man will let himself be lost for my sake, he will find his true self" (Matthew 16:25 NEB).

TA18 KATHRYN KUHLMAN — "AN HOUR WITH KATHRYN KUHLMAN"

TA19 KEVIN RANAGHAN, Author of "CATHOLIC PENTECOSTALS"

TA20 CHARLES SIMPSON — "A SOUTHERN BAPTIST LOOKS AT PENTECOST"

TA21 WILLARD CANTELON — "THE NEW WORLD MONEY SYSTEM"

TA22 THE CHARISMATIC RENEWAL —Bredesen, Ervin, Evans, Brown, Roberts

TA23 FR. JOSEPH ORSINI, Author of "HEAR MY CONFESSION"

TA24 PHIL SAINT, Author of "AMAZING SAINTS"

TA25 PAT ROBERTSON, Author of "SHOUT IF FROM THE HOUSETOPS"

TA26 MALCOLM SMITH, Author of "TURN YOUR BACK ON THE PROBLEM"

TA27 FRANK FOGLIO, Author of "HEY, GOD!"

RECORDS

MS120 AN HOUR WITH KATHRYN KUHLMAN $5.00

M7 NICKY CRUZ — 7" record $1.00

M13-72 NICKY CRUZ — 12" record $4.95

M125 NEW WORLD MONEY SYSTEM — Willard Cantelon $4.95

MS121 TAYLOR MADE CHARISMATIC MUSIC $4.95

order from your local bookstore
or W.B.S.,
Box 292
Watchung, N.J. 07061

SUGGESTED INEXPENSIVE PAPERBACK BOOKS
WHEREVER PAPERBACKS ARE SOLD
OR USE ORDER FORM

A NEW SONG—Boone	AA3	$ .95
AGLOW WITH THE SPIRIT—Frost	L326	.95
AMAZING SAINTS—Saint	L409	2.50
AND FORBID NOT TO SPEAK—Ervin	L329	.95
AND SIGNS FOLLOWED—Price	P002	1.50
ANGLES OF LIGHT?—Freeman	A506	.95
ANSWERS TO PRAISE—Carothers	L670	1.95
ARMSTRONG ERROR—DeLoach	L317	.95
AS AT THE BEGINNING—Harper	L721	.95
BAPTISM IN THE SPIRIT—Schep	L343	1.50
BAPTISM IN THE SPIRIT—BIBLICAL —Cockburn	16F	.65
BAPTISM OF FIRE—Harper	8F	.60
BAPTIZED IN ONE SPIRIT—Baker	1F	.60
BEN ISRAEL—Katz	A309	.95
BLACK TRACKS—Miles	A298	.95
BORN TO BURN—Wallace	A508	.95
CHALLENGING COUNTERFEIT—Gasson	L102	.95
COMING ALIVE—Buckingham	A501	.95
CONFESSIONS OF A HERETIC—Hunt	L31X	2.50
COUNSELOR TO COUNSELOR—Campbell	L335	1.50
CRISIS AMERICA—Otis	AA1	.95
DAYSPRING—White	L334	1.95
DISCOVERY (Booklet)—Frost	F71	.50
ERA OF THE SPIRIT—Williams	L322	1.95
15 STEPS OUT—Mumford	L106	1.50
FROM THE BELLY OF THE WHALE—White	A318	.95
GATHERED FOR POWER—Pulkingham	AA4	2.50
GOD BREAKS IN—Congdon	L313	1.95

GOD IS FOR THE EMOTIONALLY ILL —Guldseth	A507	.95
GOD'S GUERRILLAS—Wilson	A152	.95
GOD'S JUNKIE—Arguinzoni	A509	.95
GOD'S LIVING ROOM—Walker	A123	.95
GONE IS SHADOWS' CHILD—Foy	L337	.95
GRACE AND THE GLORY OF GOD —Benson/Jarman	L104	1.50
HEALING ADVENTURE—White	L345	1.95
HEALING LIGHT—Sanford	L726	.95
HEAR MY CONFESSION—Orsini	L341	1.00
HEY GOD!—Foglio	P007	1.95
HOLY SPIRIT AND YOU—Bennett	L324	2.50
JESUS AND ISRAEL—Benson	A514	.95
JESUS PEOPLE ARE COMING—King	L340	1.95
JESUS PEOPLE—Pederson	AA2	.95
LAYMAN'S GUIDE TO HOLY SPIRIT—Rea	L387	2.50
LET THIS CHURCH DIE—Weaver	A520	.95
LIFE IN THE HOLY SPIRIT—Harper	5F	.50
LONELY NOW—Cruz	A510	.95
LORD OF THE VALLEYS—Bulle	L018	2.50
LOST SHEPHERD—Sanford	L328	.95
MADE ALIVE—Price	P001	1.50
MANIFEST VICTORY—Moseley	L724	2.50
MIRACLES THROUGH PRAYER—Harrell	A518	.95
NICKY CRUZ GIVES THE FACTS ON DRUGS —Cruz	B70	.50
NINE O'CLOCK IN THE MORNING—Bennett	P555	2.50
NONE CAN GUESS—Harper	L722	1.95
OUT OF THIS WORLD—Fisher	A517	.95
OVERFLOWING LIFE—Frost	L327	1.75
PATHWAY TO POWER—Davidson	L00X	1.50
PENTECOSTALS—Nichol	LH711	2.50
PIONEERS OF REVIVAL—Clarke	L723	.95

POWER IN PRAISE—Carothers	L342	1.95
POWER FOR THE BODY—Harper	4F	.85
PREACHER WITH A BILLY CLUB—Asmuth	A209	.95
PRISON TO PRAISE—Carothers	A504	.95
PROPHECY A GIFT FOR THE BODY—Harper	2F	.65
PSEUDO CHRISTIANS—Jarman	A516	.95
REAL FAITH—Price	P000	1.50
RUN BABY RUN—Cruz	L101	.95
RUN BABY RUN—Cruz (Comic Book)		.20
SATAN SELLERS—Warnke	L794	2.50
SOUL PATROL—Bartlett	A500	.95
SPEAKING WITH GOD—Cantelon	L336	.95
SPIRIT BADE ME GO—DuPlessis	L325	.95
SPIRITUAL AND PHYSICAL HEALING —Price	P003	1.95
SPIRITUAL WARFARE—Harper	A505	.95
STRONGER THAN PRISON WALLS —Wurmbrand	A956	.95
TAKE ANOTHER LOOK—Mumford	L338	2.50
THERE'S MORE—Hall	L344	1.50
THESE ARE NOT DRUNKEN—Ervin	L105	2.50
THIS EARTH'S END—Benson	A513	.95
THIS WHICH YE SEE AND HEAR—Ervin	L728	1.95
TONGUES UNDER FIRE—Lillie	3F	.85
TURN YOUR BACK ON THE PROBLEM —Smith	L034	1.95
TWO WORLDS—Price	P004	1.95
UNDERGROUND SAINTS—Wurmbrand	U-1	.95
WALK IN THE SPIRIT—Harper	L319	.95
WE'VE BEEN ROBBED—Meloon	L339	1.50
YOU CAN KNOW GOD—Price	POO5	.75
YOUR NEW LOOK—Buckingham	A503	.95

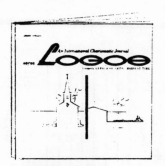

-------WHEREVER PAPERBACKS ARE SOLD OR USE THIS COUPON-------

WBS
Box 292, Plainfield, NJ 07061

SEND INSPIRATIONAL BOOKS LISTED BELOW

Title	Cat. No.	Price

☐ Send Complete Catalog

☐ Free Sample copy of the LOGOS Journal

☐ 1 year subscription LOGOS Journal $3.00. Make payment to WBS, Box 292, Plainfield, NJ 07061

Name _____

Street _____

City _____ State _____ Zip _____